THE PRACTICAL GUIDE TO BECOMING THE LEAST BORING PERSON IN THE ROOM

A COLLECTION OF STORIES TO DELIGHT AND SURPRISE

PRACTICAL GUIDES

BOOK TWO

TOM MCHALE

PRACTICAL GUIDES

INTRODUCTION

What's not to love about an interesting story? My favorites are the ones inspiring just a touch of pleasant surprise...

"Wow! I never knew that!"

With that objective in mind, I hope you enjoy this collection of seemingly random but actually thoughtfully chosen stories about the world we live in.

PART I
PEOPLE

Guests, like fish, begin to smell after 3 days.
Ben Franklin

When the eagles are silent, the parrots begin to jabber.
Winston Churchill

The problem is not the problem. The problem is your attitude about the problem.
Captain Jack Sparrow

YOU'RE SO VAIN: STRIKING A VOCAL CHORD

The Rolling Stones have made a heck of a dent in the music landscape over the past six decades. Another full-lipped and stunningly talented performer made her own ripple in music history. How about Carly Simon, writer and singer of the classic *You're So Vain*? What do these two have to do with each other? Read on...

STONES ROLL

The Stones spent the first three years of their career playing mostly other people's music, focusing on interpretations of 1950s Chicago blues. Eventually, the rebellious street-fighting men from Dartford and other English locales figured out that long-term viability as a profitable rock band would require original material. It didn't take long for the duo of Mick Jagger and Keith Richards' fledgling songwriting career to produce gold.

When 1965 happened, everything changed, and the band got all the *Sympathy (for the Devil)* they could ever ask for. If you're going to start writing your own music, you might as well produce a hit likely to remain popular for a century or so.

We could spend the night together talking Stones lore, but the fun and interesting bit is where this story intersects with rock icon Carly Simon. Some girls have all the luck, hobnobbing with one of the most iconic rock bands ever.

CARLY'S CAREER

Born just 31 days before Mick Jagger, singer, songwriter, and children's author Carly Simon was making waves of her own. OK, conspiracy theorists, among the hard-core trivia PhDs, some believe Simon was born in 1945, but we're not gonna settle that here. Most trust the '43 date, so we're sticking with that. Besides, it makes for a better story.

Anyway, she hadn't got time for the pain and cranked out a slew of stuff you might just know by heart: *Anticipation, You Belong to Me, Mockingbird, Nobody Does It Better, The Spy Who Loved Me* (a Bond theme from the movie of the same name), *Jesse* and many more.

I didn't mention *that one notable tune*, but I promise we'll get back to it in a hot second.

One quick aside about Carly. In addition to arguably being kind of the spitting image of that Jagger facial profile (my opinion only; your mileage may vary), she was also born with publishing in her blood.

Her father, also not surprisingly named "Simon," was "that" Simon—co-founder of the Simon and Schuster publishing megalopoly.

YOU'RE SO VAIN MEETING OF THE MOUTHS

Here's one of those fun facts you either know or not, but if you don't, you end up smacking your forehead and saying, "How did I not realize that before?" Whatever your answer, I ask this question nearly every time the song comes on, and to date, only a handful of folks have known this precious morsel of rock and roll trivia. First, the background...

Carly Simon released her big, big, big hit, *You're So Vain,* in November of 1972 on the album *No Secrets.* The song was huge, driving the album to a number-one spot on the Billboard 200 for five straight weeks.

Leading up to that time, Mick and the Stones would have been working on what many believe to be their finest album, *Exile on Main Street.* But somehow, during that busy time between the release of 1971's *Sticky Fingers* and recording *Exile,* he found time for an undocumented side hustle with Carly Simon. No, not that kind. At least that we know of.

Whether the duo used any *Mother's Little Helper* or not, Jagger was certainly Carly's little helper on the *No Secrets* album. What did he do?

Carly's *secret and uncredited* backup singer on her chart-busting hit, *You're So Vain,* was none other than ... rock and roll bad boy Mick Jagger.

As you listen to the song, Mr. Epic Lips comes in gently on the chorus about halfway through, perhaps at 25 percent of Carly's vocal intensity. With each subsequent chorus, Jagger's voice grows louder and stronger while Carly's fades into the background. By the end of the song, it's nearly all classic Jagger, and it is glorious. Not only do these two share more than a passing resemblance, but their voices meld like peanut butter and chocolate. Now, there's an idea; someone should market that.

Anyway, Jagger's uncredited appearance on the record was not some strategic thing designed as a PR coup. According to Simon, he just happened to call the studio where she was working on *No Secrets*, and she asked on a whim, "We're doing some backup vocals on a song of mine; why don't you come down and sing with us?" And such is the way great moments are born.

WHO'S SO VAIN?

People often wonder … who "probably thought this song was about them?"

Some point to Mick Jagger. Others Warren Beatty. Carly was mum about the lyrical target for most of her life, but in 2003, for a charity auction, she "sold" the knowledge to a lucky bidder for $50,000. That person? TV sports broadcasting mogul Dick Ebersol. But even he couldn't say as part of the condition of the sale was he couldn't share the info publicly.

In 2015, Simon came clean with part of the answer. The second verse of *You're So Vain* was about Warren Beatty, but the other verses were about two different men. The rumor mill says she's told a couple of folks—Howard Stern and Taylor Swift—but they're not talking.

WHO IS SANTA CLAUS?

Santa Claus. Saint Nick. Sinter Klaas. Pere Noel. Father Christmas. Babo Natalie. Ded Moroz. Tim Allen ran down a long list of "his" alternate names for the big man in the red suit in that scene in *The Santa Clause*. But who is Santa, really, and where did he come from?

THIRD CENTURY ORIGINS

From most accounts, St. Nicholas of Myra is the original Santa Claus. In the region now known as Turkey, Saint Nicholas was born around 270 A.D. The records of his life are sparse, and there's a better than even chance some things have been, let's say, embellished here and there. Santa is supposed to be a man of mystery, so we're OK with that.

Word is that his family died during an epidemic when he was a child, so, taking a cue from one of the many proclamations of Jesus in the Bible, he took to heart the advice to "sell his possessions and give the money to the poor." Nicholas proceeded to use his inheritance to help the needy and downtrodden. In short order, from his relentless service to others and the church, he was named the Bishop of Myra.

THE ULTIMATE PATRON SAINT

Saint Nicholas is the patron saint of children, which makes a lot of sense, given he's the original Kris Kringle. However, he's the patron saint of many other folks, too. He's also known as the patron saint of sailors and those who work around the sea. And of brides, bakers, bankers, firefighters, judges, merchants, millers and spinsters. And we're just getting started. If you're a prisoner, preacher, poet, pharmacist, or perfumer, Saint Nicholas is your guy. And don't forget pawnbrokers, rag pickers, thieves and newlyweds. We're still just getting started; there are well over a hundred other benefactor groups of Nicholas' sainthood.

SAINT NICHOLAS DAY

Again, considering the limitations of sparse historical records, Saint Nicholas died on December 6, 343 A.D. While the exact year may be under some dispute, lots of folks have celebrated December 6 as Saint Nicholas Day for a few hundred years now. Near the end of the 18th century, a New York paper ran a story about Dutch families celebrating Saint Nick's death, thereby beginning the process of linking Saint Nicholas with the Christmas season.

SINTER KLAAS... SANTA CLAUS...

Those Dutch folks, particularly keen on the Saint Nicholas celebrations, called him Sint Nikolaas. The familiar short abbreviation is "Sinterklaas." And there we have it—the likely origin of the English term, Santa Claus.

ABOUT THE GIFTS...

There are lots of stories documenting Saint Nicholas' generosity and selflessness. One such story sheds light on the whole idea of a secret nice guy smuggling gifts *into* our homes.

A poor resident of Nicholas' town had three daughters. At that time, families had to offer a dowry to prospective husbands to entice them into marriage. With no prospect of saving up suitable dowries, the daughters' future included being sold into slavery and possibly prostitution. Hey, don't blame the messenger; I'm just telling the story.

On three different occasions, as the daughters reached suitable marriage age, "someone" anonymously tossed bags of gold through the windows of the poor man's home. According to legend, these gifts to the family landed in shoes and stockings drying in front of the fire. Hmm. Gifts secretly delivered into stockings. Sound familiar?

WAS MR. ROGERS A NAVY SEAL? MYTH VS. REALITY OF AMERICA'S FAVORITE CHILDREN'S SHOW HOST

Mr. Rogers, affectionately known as Fred Rogers to his SEAL teammates, grew bored of the early advisory role he and his fellow SEALS had in the Vietnam War. He singlehandedly spearheaded the program of short-term rotation of 12-14-man platoons of SEALS for direct action in country, culminating in his personal development of the "men in green faces" legend and the highly effective Operation Phoenix program. After receiving seven Medals of Honor,

Rogers agreed to make room for new SEAL team members and resigned his commission to launch a successful children's television empire. In between, he founded the 1st Special Forces Operational Detachment-Delta (1st SFOD-D) unit. You can take the warrior out of the war, but not the war out of the warrior. As for the famed children's show, Mr. Rogers' Neighborhood, that was all just a charade to keep a lid on his top-secret, brutal combat record.

OK, so absolutely none of that is true, but somehow, the myth of Mr. Rogers, tough guy extraordinaire, lives on. Other versions of the story place him behind the rifle as a Marine Scout Sniper. You have to admit, one seriously intriguing narrative is the possibility of America's gentlest and most polite television personality having a hidden life as a fierce warrior. It could make a movie that rivals the masterful combination of humor, fantasy, and action of *True Lies*.

For you younger parents, Mr. Rogers' Neighborhood is a genuine classic and the inspiration for today's Daniel Tiger's Neighborhood.

MR. ROGERS MYTHS... BUSTED

Born on March 20, 1928, Fred Rogers grew up to be an ordained Presbyterian minister. However, he chose to lead by example rather than publicly talk about his faith on his television platform.

As for the military service myth, many believe that it arose from the Presidential Medal of Freedom awarded to him by President George W. Bush. That medal doesn't imply any military connection; Irving Berlin, Jacques Cousteau and Maya Angelou were awarded the same.

Part two of the myth originates from Mr. Roger's trademark long-sleeved sweaters. Keyboard warriors have it on good authority that Mr. Rogers wore those to cover all the tattoos he had applied during his military service, although none have actually seen his bare arms.

I suppose Fred Rogers would have been one busy man, maintaining his kill stats in Vietnam while filming his show, which aired from 1968 to 2001. Those early morning risers sure can pack a lot into a day, can't they?

A MILITARY CONNECTION

Fred Rogers did have a tangential connection to things military. He developed a close relationship with family friend George Allen. George was a military pilot who served as an instructor in the famed Tuskegee Air Force, eventually being promoted to chief instructor of pilot cadets at Tuskegee Army Air Field in 1941.

Before his time molding fighter pilots at Tuskegee, Allen taught Rogers to fly during his high school years.

REAL FACTS ABOUT MR. ROGERS

He was as humble in real life as we saw during the show and often asked permission to photograph new acquaintances, saying, "I like to take pictures of my new friends."

Those famous sweaters were knitted by his mother, Nancy, who relentlessly produced the famous zippered cardigans at the rate of one per month until her death in 1981. After that, his art director ordered similar sweaters and dyed them in fun colors. Interestingly, Fred Rogers was red-green colorblind.

Mr. Rogers received an average of 50-100 fan letters daily—and answered them all. When you get up at 5:30 every morning to a mug of hot cranberry juice, you make time for such essential tasks.

There was a character trait Mr. Rogers had in common with the SEAL mentality. While on a far lower scale, he did share a lifelong commitment to physical fitness, swimming every morning to maintain his ideal weight of 143 pounds. But even for that, Mr. Rogers applied his trademark lesson for the kids. To him, 143 represents "I love you." I (one letter), love (four letters), and you (three letters).

It's still a beautiful day in the neighborhood, isn't it?

WALK THIS WAY ... LITERALLY

Aerosmith's 1975 not-as-big-of-an-initial-hit-as-it-would-later-become, *Walk This Way,* almost didn't see the light of day. It wasn't for lack of trying; it was more a result of the band's early struggles with writing lyrics. The song wasn't pre-written for recording. Rather, it was an impromptu effort that later became the second single release from Aerosmith's 1975 album, *Toys in the Attic*. Since you might now be wondering, the lead single on the album was *Sweet Emotion*.

WALK THIS WAY'S ORIGIN STORY

Aerosmith lead guitarist Joe Perry came up with that punchy electric guitar riff while doing a sound check for a performance in Honolulu, Hawaii, back in 1974. At that time, the fledging band scored a gig as the opening act for *The Guess Who*. While tinkering with riffs while the sound engineers and roadies did their thing, Perry came up with the now-iconic *Walk This Way* rapid-fire guitar lick. By the end of the sound check, the song, sans lyrics, was mostly roughed out.

HARD WORDS

Fast forward to 1975, and the band was recording *Toys in the Attic* at the Record Plant in New York City. One problem. They only had a handful of songs ready to go, so the remainder had to be written in the studio. Nothing inspires urgency quite like doing your homework on the bus ride to school.

Still needing a punchy, upbeat number, Perry resurrected his riff from the Honolulu sound check. Steven Tyler got into it, and like he did in Hawaii, scatting nonsense lyrics to find the groove.

Enter writer's block. Tyler had an insanely high internal standard for his work. Good lyrics must not only make sense and support the song but also accentuate the music. As a drummer by trade, many of Tyler's lyrics are percussive in nature, adding another "instrument" in effect. And Tyler had a thing for taking double-entendre to the extreme. He always wanted to take his songs right to the edge of getting banned from radio. This compulsion threw yet another lyrical roadblock in the way.

Net-net: no luck on lyrics. The group was at an impasse.

COMEDIC RELIEF

Doing what all good producers do, Jack Douglas joined the band for a much-needed break, heading to Times Square to see the new Mel Brooks movie, *Young Frankenstein*. Tyler had already seen the movie, so he remained at the studio.

Later, the group headed back in high spirits, laughing and replaying the classic line, "Walk this way…" Igor (pronounced eye-gore), played by Marty Feldman, asks Dr. Frankenstein (pronounced fronk-en-steen), played by Gene Wilder, to follow him by "walking this way." Igor dutifully hands Frankenstein his walking stick, so Wilder can limp away from the train station, as does the hunchback. Hey, you have to see it. It was funny.

All are laughing at the Three Stooges-like comedy, and Jack suggests, "Hey, 'Walk this way' might be a great title for the song." All agree, and Tyler goes to work, agreeing to finish the words at his hotel that night.

Speaking of Gene Wilder, did you know he laid down a condition for accepting the role of the original Willy Wonka? It was his idea for the first glimpse of the Candy King to show him hobbling to the factory gate using a cane, tripping, and diving into a comedic fall and roll. Wilder figured that would set the stage for the audience never knowing whether Wonka was lying or telling the truth. Some people just have the vision, don't they?

MY CAB ATE IT

Anyway, back to New York the following morning. Tyler swears he completed the *Walk This Way* lyrics in his hotel the night before but must have left them in the cab. Crunch time. Donning headphones and a portable tape player, he disappeared into a remote stairwell in the Record Plant, listening to Perry's music and starting fresh on the lyrics.

Realizing he had forgotten paper, Tyler wrote the words on the stairwell wall, transcribing them later. You can't interrupt the creative process.

HAPPY ENDING

Tyler cranked out the lyrics in a couple of hours. The band recorded the song, and in 1977, it made the top 10.

The development of the song itself makes for a pretty good story, but what happened later sets the stage for another. Arguably, what really gave *Walk This Way* a long-term impact was how it helped bridge the musical divide between rock and rap. In 1985, Run D.M.C. producer Rick Rubin brought the two bands together to create and perform a full rap version of the proto-rap tune, once again rocketing *Walk This Way* into the top 10.

Give the Run D.M.C. — Aerosmith video a watch. It's not exactly subtle about the message of breaking down the wall between two diverse styles of music, but it sure is entertaining.

PEOPLE WHO CHANGED HISTORY: LT. COMMANDER JOHN WALDRON & TORPEDO SQUADRON 8

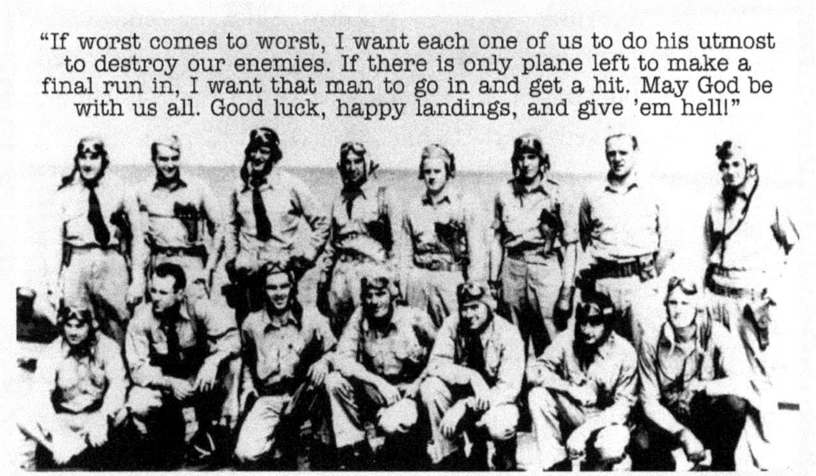
"If worst comes to worst, I want each one of us to do his utmost to destroy our enemies. If there is only plane left to make a final run in, I want that man to go in and get a hit. May God be with us all. Good luck, happy landings, and give 'em hell!"

The Battle of Midway on June 4, 1942, marks one of those moments in history where small (in the scope of things) acts and decisions literally turned the course of history on its ear. In fact, the Battle of Midway is chock full of decisions and acts by a few among those of the thousands involved that shaped not only the outcome of the battle but that of World War II and life as we know it today. Would the United States exist today with a different outcome?

Probably, but things might be very different. The story of Lt. Commander John Waldron and Torpedo Squadron 8 is one such extraordinary tale.

> If worst comes to worst, I want each one of us to do his utmost to destroy our enemies. If there is only one plane left to make a final run in, I want that man to go in and get a hit. May God be with us all. Good luck, happy landings, and give 'em hell!
>
> *Lt. Commander John Waldron, USN*

THE BATTLE OF MIDWAY: DO OR DIE TIME.

Six months after the attack on Pearl Harbor, the United States Navy was still reeling from the aftermath as a large part of the Pacific Fleet was damaged or sunk. Of the eight battleships present, all were damaged, and four were sunk. Other Navy ships were damaged or sunk, nearly 200 aircraft were destroyed, and over 2,400 military personnel were killed. Pearl Harbor put a serious dent in the United States' ability to wage war across millions of square miles of the Pacific theater.

TRAP VS. COUNTER-TRAP...

Admiral Yamamoto of the Japanese Navy knew he had to execute a follow-up attack after Pearl Harbor, but with the influx of people, ships and planes, a second attack at a later date was deemed too risky. Instead, he correctly calculated the US would vigorously defend a tiny Island, Midway, located nearly 1,500 miles from Hawaii because it was considered a vital outpost. By attacking there, Yamamoto hoped to draw US forces away from heavily protected Hawaii, where he could crush the US Fleet.

SNAP! I BROKE YOUR CODE!

Meanwhile, dedicated codebreakers in Honolulu, led by one Commander Joseph Rochefort, had figured out how to decode secure Japanese messages, or at least enough of them to understand future operational plans. The team knew something was in the works regarding a US installation the Japanese referred to as "AF." In an elaborate ruse, the US Navy fabricated a story about a broken water purification system on Midway and transmitted a message to Pearl Harbor saying they had water troubles. The code breakers soon intercepted a Japanese communication saying, "AF was short on water."

Target confirmed. The US Navy now had the opportunity to set a countertrap in the vicinity of Midway Island.

THE BATTLE OF MIDWAY

Many know of the Battle of Midway on June 4, 1942. Some might also know that it marked the turning point of the war in the Pacific. On that day, three squadrons of SBD scout bombers from the aircraft carriers Enterprise and Yorktown dove on the Japanese fleet and put the Japanese Kaga, Akagi, and Soryu carriers permanently out of action. Later that day, American carrier-based planes sank a fourth carrier—the Hiryu.

What is not so well known are the amazing circumstances that led to the United States Navy turning the tide of the war by permanently ending Japan's near-total dominance of the Pacific.

JOHN WALDRON'S TORPEDO SQUADRON 8

During the early stages of the battle, Lt. Commander John Waldron led Torpedo Squadron 8 straight into the jaws of the Japanese fleet, completely unescorted by fighter cover. This was a big deal. The torpedo bombers were big, slow, lumbering aircraft with virtually no chance of protecting themselves against the nimble and advanced Japanese Zero fighter aircraft. Normally, torpedo bombers would be escorted by fighters and other attacking high-altitude bombers so they wouldn't have to go against enemy fighters alone. Waldron and his men didn't wait for help—they commenced the attack regardless.

Japanese Zero fighter aircraft, providing protection for the fleet high above, found the temptation of attacking the defenseless American torpedo planes irresistible and quickly descended from high altitude to sea level to stop the torpedo attack.

Lt. Commander Waldron's entire squadron was destroyed by the fast and maneuverable Zeros. Every single plane was shot down. Worse yet, not one managed to get close enough to the Japanese fleet to score a single hit.

A TRAGIC, BUT BATTLE-ALTERING SACRIFICE

However, what appeared to be a complete and total sacrifice without result by Lt. Commander John Waldron and those brave American pilots would arguably change the outcome of the war. As the Zero fighters, now at sea level, finished off Torpedo Squadron 8, the three squadrons of SBD scout bombers arrived high above and commenced their attack, completely unopposed by the now out-of-range Zero fighters. Within minutes, three Japanese aircraft carriers were burning out of control, and the tide of the war had changed forever.

What initially appeared to be a senseless waste of the men and machines of Torpedo Squadron 8 proved to be the factor that helped the dive bomber attack succeed, leading to the near destruction of Japanese naval air power. After that, the Japanese were never able to adequately resupply the lost ships and crews, allowing the Americans to ultimately prevail.

SARAH AND THE WINCHESTER MYSTERY HOUSE

You know what's a real bummer? When you embark on some loony ritual, suggested by a kooky medium to prolong your own life or perhaps instill immortality, and you faithfully execute that recommended "health" plan with vigor your entire life until you… die. That's the sad story of Sarah Winchester and the Winchester Mystery House. Yeah, you might recognize the name. She was heiress to the famed small arms company that arguably helped "win the West."

History hasn't been kind to poor Sarah, with most people believing she was a nutcase.

The gist of the story goes like this... Freaked out by the loss of her only daughter, followed by the death of her husband some years later, Sarah moved out west to San Jose. There, she embarked on a lifelong project of building the world's weirdest funhouse mansion, all to confuse and deter the angry spirits of those killed by Winchester's small arms. Or something like that.

That's the story, but is it true?

THE PLAYERS

William Wirt Winchester was the son of Oliver Winchester, founder of the Winchester Repeating Arms company. Rising to the position of company treasurer, William was the guy next in line to control the successful arms maker. In 1862, William married Sarah Lockwood Pardee and four years later, they had their only child. Tragically, the baby died just six weeks later.

In 1880, Oliver Winchester passed away, leaving the company primarily in the hands of William. But in 1881, tragedy struck again, and William died of tuberculosis. Sarah, now Sarah Winchester, was left with a chunk of ownership in the small arms empire.

Suffering from health issues of her own and perhaps a desperate need for a change of scenery given all the tragic events, Sarah moved west to San Jose, California, buying up an eight-room farmhouse on a 45-acre plot, promptly naming it Llanada Villa.

Here's where things started to get a little weird.

FACT OR FICTION?

As the always reliable rumor mill goes, and stamped with a seal of approval (insert sarcasm here) from the Hollywood motion picture *Winchester*, Sarah had received a $20 million inheritance and control of the Winchester company upon the death of her husband, William.

As most grieving heiresses do, Sarah immediately consulted a medium, who planted the seed of an idea that all the ghosts of those killed by Winchester rifles were sticking around just to torment Sarah. Her best defense against these spirit skirmishes was to embark on a frantic and never-ceasing construction program to convert Llanada Villa into a maze slash jail for spirits. Ghosts would wander, get lost and eventually become trapped in the labyrinth of hallways, staircases and rooms. I can see the logic...

THE WINCHESTER MYSTERY HOUSE

So, from 1886 to 1922, Sarah oversaw daily construction and renovation of her home. The original eight-room farmhouse expanded into a sprawling 160-room monument to excess. At its peak, the mansion reportedly had 500 rooms.

Arguably the world's weirdest house, this one contains 24,000 feet of interior space, accessible through 2,000 doors and separated from the outside world by 10,000 windows. Skylights? 52. Stairways? 47. Bathrooms? Only 13, which seems a bit light for all those rooms, but who are we to judge? At least the home housed six kitchens, so one wouldn't have to sleepwalk too far for a midnight snack.

Over the 38 years of on-and-off construction, Sarah assumed architectural responsibilities herself, taking on the project as a life mission. According to the craftsmen employed, she was exceptionally "hands-on" for each room built. If a new addition didn't turn out as envisioned, Sarah was known to tear it out and start over. Word has it that one project was restarted 16 times.

All this tinkering resulted in an "interesting" if disjointed overall design. The stopping and starting left strange features like staircases ending in a ceiling, doors that lead to nowhere, and windows covered by interior walls. One famous feature is the world's shallowest staircase, with 44 steps rising just 10 feet.

THE TRUTH?

A good story often takes on a life of its own. Add the financial incentives of a popular tourist attraction from 1923 until the present day, a Hollywood horror flick for accent, and you have plenty of reason to embellish the facts just a bit.

Some of the lore is easy to disprove or at least question. When William Winchester died, his estate was valued at around $370,000, little of which was available to Sarah at the time. William's mother controlled the majority interest in the company until 1898. Still, Sarah certainly wasn't poor by any means.

As for the creepy supernatural stuff, there's little evidence for much of it being true. Friends and family claim Sarah had no discernible paranormal interests. Rather, she viewed her personal construction empire as more of a hobby to express her artistic creations, which grew to an obligation of sorts to keep local carpenters and craftsmen employed.

As for the dead-end doors and hallways, perhaps chalk that up to Sarah's stop-and-start modus operandi. And the steps? Sarah measured just four feet, ten inches and was in declining health. Cautious ride operators might have discouraged her from riding Space Mountain. Is it that strange you'd build custom staircases to support your physical limitations?

The Winchester Mystery House (allegedly named thusly by none other than Harry Houdini) still operates as a tourist attraction. So, if you are in the area, check it out. Just take the stories with a grain of salt. More than one former tour guide has expressed regret at having to repeat, let's say, embellishments about Sarah Winchester's tragic life.

SUSPICIOUS MINDS EXPLORE ELVIS PRESLEY, THE KING OF ROCK AND ROLL

Not too long ago, we shared the surprisingly little-known story of how Mick Jagger and Carly Simon collaborated on one of the more popular songs of all time. Now it's time to shift gears and explore a few interesting facts about a different sort of rock icon. Ahh, the King.

While he didn't quite intersect with my own peak musical interest era, it's hard for anyone to deny his impact on the genre of Rock and

Roll. Just so we're on the same page, we're talking about Elvis Presley, the King of Rock and Roll. Now, how about *A Little Less Conversation* so we can get to the story?

A GIFT FOR MOM

Growing up shy, Elvis Presley had a close relationship with his mom. His interest in music led him not only to learn the guitar while growing up but also to become a record shop groupie, stopping by Charlie's Record Shop in Memphis frequently to listen to the newest music. Record stores are a gateway drug, especially for those with enough passion to learn instruments without lessons. Soon, Elvis upped his fixation to the Sun Records recording studio run by one Sam Phillips.

In August 1953, Elvis recorded a song called *My Happiness* as a gift for dear old mom. Over the months, Sam, while remaining largely unimpressed, hooked the future king up with a couple of other musicians, Bill Black and Scotty Moore. The trio recorded some songs, but nothing came of it.

ELVIS PRESLEY'S LITERAL BREAK

If you have ever seen the movie *That Thing You Do!*, which documents the fictional discovery, rise, and fall of a 1964 rock group, The Oneders (pronounced 'wonders' by the band until savvy producer Tom Hanks made them change their name to 'The Wonders'), you might remember the pivotal scene. Last-minute replacement drummer Guy Patterson forces the group into an on-stage faster and more upbeat tempo version of the ballad they intended to play for a local talent show. The improv version of the song, more "rock-like," is an instant hit, and the group takes off.

Whether the movie draws from Elvis's pivotal move is debatable, but his discovery followed a similar path. While the trio was on a break at Sun Records, Elvis sang an impromptu, faster and more "Elvis-like" version of a blues song called *That's All Right*. You can guess the rest. Scotty and Bill join in with bass and guitar. Sam records the song, and a few days later, it's on the radio. The rest is history.

THE WORLD'S GREATEST NON-SONG WRITER

While the myth persists that Elvis Presley couldn't really play the guitar, the fact is he was just kinda humble about his guitar skills. Not having formal lessons and learning his skills by ear, he almost always had a guitar by his side from age ten when he completed his first public performance.

Likely, the "I don't play the guitar" story was supported by his various comments in interviews over the years. For example, during an October 28, 1957 interview in Los Angeles, when asked if he read music, Elvis responded, "No. And I can't play the guitar, either." When asked what he did with his guitar if he didn't play it, Elvis responded, "I use it as a brace."

Sorry, but now we have to check into the *Heartbreak Hotel*. There is some peripheral truth in here about Elvis's musical talent. While the king of rock and roll recorded some 600 songs over his career, he never wrote one himself. *Don't Be Cruel*; great performers are a legitimate art form on their own. The great Elton John maintains a lifelong partnership with lyrics songwriter Bernie Taupin. During that same interview, the topic was explored further.

"It's all a big hoax, honey. I never wrote a song in my life. I get one-third of the credit for recording it. It makes me look smarter than I am. I've never even had an idea for a song. Just once, maybe… I went to bed one night, had quite a dream, and woke up all shook up. I phoned a pal and told him about it. By morning, he had a new song, '*All Shook Up*'."

DOUBLE TROUBLE: THE PRESIDENTIAL ORIGIN OF "OK"

One U.S. President has a double dose of party trivia. OK, let's start with this teaser. Who was the first president born in the United States?

Here's a hint. It's none of the names likely come to mind. Washington? Nope. How about Jefferson? Not him, either. Madison? Good guess, but ... nah. And it wasn't John Adams either. Then, it must be

John Quincy Adams. Wrong again. That's OK; most people get this question wrong if they hurry to the more obvious answers.

THE FIRST PRESIDENT BORN IN THE UNITED STATES

The answer is… the 8th president of the United States, Martin Van Buren, who reigned, sorry, represented American Citizens from 1837 to 1841.

OK, it was a bit of a trick question. Thomas Jefferson, George Washington, and James Madison were born in Virginia. John and John Quincy Adams were both born in Massachusetts. So, what's the problem?

When all five of them were born, along with James Monroe and Andrew Jackson, the United States didn't exist. That didn't happen until July 4, 1776, when the colonies severed ties with Great Britain.

So, Martin Van Buren was the first President who was actually born "in" the United States.

OK, WHAT ELSE?

If you're tuned in to frivolous word games, you might have noticed we've used the term "OK" a lot in this article—with good reason.

You see, Martin Van Buren, in addition to being the original American President, is credited, at least partially, with the now universal term "OK." His birthplace was Kinderhook, New York, and over time, folks started using the friendly nickname of "Old Kinderhook." Hold that thought.

In 1839, the Boston Morning Post published an article dissing another paper, and in the text, wrote an abbreviation of "o.k." near the article's use of the phrase "all correct." Back at that time, people apparently found humor in deliberately misspelled words and resulting abbreviations. Perhaps the "o.k." initials referred to "oll korrect" or something along those lines.

Fast forward to 1840, when Van Buren was running for reelection. As they always do in presidential election campaigns, things got ugly, and Team William Henry Harrison began to bandy about less-than-flattering names for Van Buren. In response, Van Buren's campaign strategists started using the "O.K." phrase, already starting to gain some traction as a play on both the "Old Kinderhook" nickname and the "oll korrect" joke from the Boston Morning Post article.

Nothing creates momentum like a presidential campaign, so the term "OK" took off, meaning then, as it does today, everything is hunky dory.

PART II
BUSINESS

No business school graduate would recommend gambling as a financial strategy, but sometimes it pays to be a little crazy early in your career.

Fred Smith, Founder, FedEx

Age is just a number for me—I haven't thought about it in years. I go by the motto that I learn something new every single day.

Bernard Marcus, cofounder, Home Depot

THE GREAT FEDEX GAMBLE: WHEN YOU ABSOLUTELY, POSITIVELY NEED A PILE OF MONEY OVERNIGHT

Wealthy entrepreneurs ignite more controversy than removing the Drinks on Demand program for the U.S. House of Representatives. Some feel the wealth generated by successful business movers and shakers is "unfair," while others point out that new businesses are risky and justify the potential future reward. Roughly 65% of start-up companies fail within 10 years. Over 20% go down in flames during their first year.

With each business failure, you can usually assume a corresponding personal financial disaster, including loss of life savings, homes, and massive future debt. Those who succeed are almost always marked with incredible work and perseverance stories associated with their founders.

Want to start a successful company? Be prepared to risk everything, work seven days a week for years or decades, and who knows, you might succeed and one day listen to people who think your wealth is unfair. Sometimes, the stories behind the scenes are straight out of a Hollywood movie. Consider the epic Delorean cocaine caper and the blackjack hands that built Federal Express.

FREDDIE'S STORY

Fred Smith attended Yale in the 60s, where he authored a paper on the need for reliable overnight delivery in the burgeoning Information Age. As the story goes, he got a "C" on the paper as his professor found the idea "improbable." Not to be smacked down by some classroom quarterback, Smith founded FedEx in 1971 after a couple of tours in Vietnam, where he carefully observed how large-scale logistics worked.

Some 14 small jets and 25 cities of overnight small package delivery service later, the company was off and running. But big ideas are tough to convert to profits. By 1973, the company had millions in debt and about $5,000 in the bank. With a $24,000 fuel bill due the following week, FedEx was a sure bust. No fuel, no flying, no package delivery. End of yet another entrepreneurial dream.

DESPERATE TIMES CALL FOR DESPERATE MEASURES

Apparently, Smith had developed reasonable poker skills somewhere along the way and, in a fit of pure desperation with nothing to lose, withdrew the $5,000 in cash and headed to Vegas.

Sitting down at the Blackjack tables (not poker, but let's assume some gambling skills translate), Smith managed to parlay the five grand into about $27,000.

THE REST OF THE STORY

The fuel bill gets paid, leaving about $3,000 in the bank for the next payroll. The risk-it-all gambit gave Fred Smith enough days of company life support to negotiate another $11 million in restructured loans and new financing.

By the late 1970s, the company was profitable and well on its way to its current $75 billion market value. Along the way, Smith proved the concept of reliable overnight delivery—worldwide. If I were Smith and in a particularly bratty mood, I would have sent (overnight, of course) a copy of that original paper to that Yale professor for a second look.

WANT FRIES WITH THAT?

You've gotta love a clever marketing story. Being a lifelong marketing guy myself, I tend to believe good marketing is more about actions, products and services than catchy slogans and pretty pictures.

In fact, one "marketing" executive's "marketing campaign" involved construction. Determined to find where the company could add more customer value, he watched his hotel chain's customers struggle to drag those then-new collapsible dollies for suitcase transport up the front door steps to their lobbies.

The "marketing" solution was to install ramps to make life easier for weary travelers. Brilliant. No catchy slogans required. The result was dramatic. It didn't take the travel cognoscenti long to flock to the hotels that had installed those thoughtful ramps.

GOT TIRES?

Of course, the granddaddy of all "marketing" stories involves bougie retailer Nordstrom. For those not familiar, the stores are high-end department style, chock full of fancy clothes, perfumes, jewelry and similar fare for the more well-heeled among us. As you'd expect, you'll find inside the world's supply of courteous and professional sales staff.

As the story goes, a customer walked into a Nordstrom location in Fairbanks, Alaska, toting a set of tires. Yes. Fairbanks, Alaska. And also, yes, tires. Nordstrom has never and will never sell anything involving tires. Yet the customer swore he bought them at Nordstrom and was told he could return them at any time. Fast forward a few minutes. The manager called a local tire shop to get a value estimate and promptly refunded the customer in cash.

Most assume the story is an urban myth, cobbled up to reflect Nordstrom's hard-earned reputation for above and beyond customer service. But one Pete Nordstrom, yes, that Pete Nordstrom, verified the story. He tracked down the employee who handled the transaction and was assured it really happened. Lost to history is the amount of the refund.

WANT FRIES WITH THAT?

A more current and subtle but effective marketing success story comes to us courtesy of Five Guys. You know, the burger joint that's popped up somewhere around 1,500 restaurants as of 2024.

If you've been to Five Guys, perhaps you've noticed the "sloppy" way someone spills fries in the bottom of your bag. Perhaps you've even complained to management about the fry mess in the bag. Many Five Guys customers have.

Guess what? The company does this on purpose. After filling the fry container, they make sure to "spill" some extra in the bag to make it look like you were served an abundance of fries—more than could even fit in the container. Of course, it's all factored into the price, but you have to admire the creativity.

Marketing. It's not just for graphic artists and copywriters.

THE DELOREAN: HOW A COCAINE DEAL ENABLED BACK TO THE FUTURE

The DeLorean DMC-12, while not a screaming performer on the track, is one of the most iconic cars of the 20th century. Its all-stainless steel and no-paint exterior make it the perfect vehicle for Hollywood fantasy science, as demonstrated by the *Back to the Future* movie franchise. What other car is such a born natural for a Time Machine that blasts through the space-time continuum when it hits precisely 88 mph?

Here's the kicker. If not for desperation to keep a struggling car company afloat, overly ambitious FBI agents, an informant with a grudge and a suitcase of cocaine, *Back to the Future* might have been one more movie headed to Blockbuster shelves far too quickly.

JOHN DELOREAN: AUTOMOTIVE ROCK STAR

John Zachary DeLorean grew up with cars in his blood. His father was a union organizer at Ford Motor Company, and John's first real job was at Chrysler, followed quickly by a short but successful career at Packard Motor Company. General Motors caught wind of the automotive engineering prodigy and recruited him, where he ran development programs for muscle cars like the Pontiac GTO, Firebird and Grand Prix. Before long, he became the youngest division chief in GM history.

DeLorean left in 1973 to build his own car—The DeLorean DMC-12.

THE "SO-SO" DELOREAN DMC-12

While it looks spiffy, the car was somewhat of a dud, leading to lackluster sales by the time it was introduced in 1982. It wasn't very fast, but at least it featured poor handling. Toss in some manufacturing and quality problems, and sales dribbled.

Then there was the creeping price tag. Originally planned at $12,000, it skyrocketed to over $30,000 by 1982. Remember, this was back when station wagons roamed the earth, so a $30,000 car was more like a six-figure set of wheels today. Ultimately, some 9,200 were made, but only a couple thousand were sold.

Like many entrepreneurs, DeLorean begged and borrowed to get the company and an Irish manufacturing plant going. A down market and weak reviews shrunk incoming cash flows, and before long, DeLorean was desperate for a lot of cash—at least $17 million. That's about $55 million today.

DRUG DEALS FOR QUICK CASH

In mid-1982, DeLorean was approached by a potential investor, James Hoffman. One minor complication: Hoffman was a convicted drug smuggler turned informant. He was somewhat motivated to land a big fish for prosecution to help save his own skin. Hoffman pursued DeLorean relentlessly with promises of investors who could help save the struggling car company, and preliminary discussions continued.

Come October, Hoffman and DeLorean were inching toward a deal. DeLorean flew to Los Angeles and met with Hoffman and someone who turned out to be an undercover FBI agent. After some discussion, a suitcase with some 55 pounds of cocaine was plopped on the table as proof of a lot more to come. Yes, the "investors" were in the business of importing cocaine.

The idea was DeLorean would invest a few million for a "buy" in South America, and everyone would get rich when the product ultimately sold in the States. Sales of this import deal would raise tens of millions, which, after various cuts among the players, would net DeLorean enough money to save his company.

The meeting could have ended a bit better for DeLorean, as he was arrested while still on the hotel property for narcotics trafficking.

HE SAID, SHE SAID...

Fast forward to 1984 and the trial...

DeLorean's defense team claimed big-time entrapment and produced some evidence of such, including claims of him sending an "if I don't make it back from this meeting in Los Angeles" letter to his attorney before the meeting.

He testified throughout the trial he was "playing along" out of fear. Then, testimony from a government agent or two illuminated the desperation to nail DeLorean, even to the point of fudging some evidence and court testimony. And there were claims of threats against DeLorean's family should he elect not to participate in the scheme.

On the flip side, there are some damning clips on video of DeLorean talking about how the stuff on the table was "better than gold" and a champagne toast wishing "a lot of success for everyone."

And then there was the fact that DeLorean had a lot to hide and he was desperate. He'd been plagued by accusations of financial mismanagement and improper spending of company money, so his potential willingness to participate in such a deal was not at all surprising. He was in a kettle of hot water, no doubt.

Only the jury knows... Guilty or not, DeLorean was acquitted by reason of illegal entrapment, but the car company was doomed, having declared bankruptcy back in 1982.

YOU CAN'T BUY THIS KIND OF PUBLICITY

Whatever the real truth about the DeLorean Drug Debacle, *Back to the Future* producers and current DeLorean owners should be thankful for the timing that swayed the movie makers' props decisions. The car itself, the global publicity of the company's struggles, DeLorean's flamboyant lifestyle, and, of course, the drug trial of the decade made the DeLorean the natural choice for Doc Brown's homemade Time Machine. What movie marketing machine wouldn't jump on all that free publicity just waiting to be exploited?

As a quick side note, early drafts of the movie scripts called for Doc Brown's Time Machine to be constructed from an old refrigerator, but producers quickly discarded that plan as potentially dangerous. If the movie turned into a hit, they didn't want kids climbing into old appliances to play "Time Machine."

It didn't take long for the idea of using a car to take hold, just as the DeLorean occupied the news cycle. Director and co-writer Bob Zemeckis is credited with the idea of using a car to go "back in time." As the story goes, Ford even offered a pile of money to make the Time Machine from a Mustang, but co-creator Bob Gale nixed that idea, exclaiming, "Doc Brown doesn't drive a &^$#&* Mustang!"

While things didn't end well for DeLorean himself, they did work out pretty well for his car. As we now know, that wire-wrapped Delorean is now one of the most iconic movie props ever.

FLYING YOUR BUTT OFF: THE LONGEST PLANE FLIGHT EVER

I don't know about you, but I start to get cranky on any airline flight lasting more than about 12 minutes.

Once, and I freely admit this pales in comparison to you far east travelers, I flew direct from Chicago to Hawaii. As I recall, that non-stop flight was about 11 hours of sheer unadulterated misery. The middle seat likely had something to do with that. Then again, all aircraft seats are girdle devices these days. I'm still in counseling. But that's nothing compared to direct flights planned by Qantas Airlines. They're launching non-stop service from London or New York to Sydney in the next year or so. That'll take nearly a day, as in 24 hours, in the air. Ouch.

But all these are lame compared to the flight made by Robert Timm and John Cook back in 1958. The longest flight ever, without landing, was…are you ready… 64 days, 22 hours, and 19 minutes. Yes, you read that right.

Here's the story.

NOTHING IS TOO WEIRD FOR LOCAL ADVERTISING

We're all accustomed to seeing the ridiculous lengths businesses will go to for local commercials. While personal injury attorneys are willing to do almost anything to make the 1-800-SLE-AZEY line ring, the Hacienda Hotel and Casino set an all-time record for sheer commitment to the promotional gimmick.

Back in 1956, Judy and "Doc" Bailey built the Hacienda Hotel and Casino on the southern end of the Vegas strip, where Mandalay Bay now resides. Looking for a creative way to promote the family-friendly resort, Bailey was intrigued by an idea from his slot machine technician, a former World War II bomber pilot named Bob Timm.

Timm convinced the Baileys to gain national publicity by breaking the world record for the longest continuous flight ever, which currently held firm at 47 days. After project funding of $100,000 in 1950s dollars (about a million today), Timm was off and ~~running~~ flying.

Step one: get a plane worthy of running for months nonstop.

Step two: find a copilot loony enough to commit to the venture. That turned out to be one John Wayne Cook.

DA PLANE!

What aeronautical marvel can remain in flight for just shy of 65 straight days? Why America's favorite private plane, of course, the storied Cessna 172. Manufactured from 1956 until, well, we'll find out should they ever stop production, this single-engine four-seater has earned its place as the most produced private aircraft in history.

Let's be clear about the "four-seater" thing. It seats four, kind of like how a phone booth (remember those?) fits three NFL offensive tackles inside. You can do it, but not without post-event counseling. Even with the two planned pilots (remember they had to fly 24 hours a day indefinitely), space was cramped, so Timm worked with a mechanic on a series of modifications. Back seats? Gone, and the space was converted to a mini mattress, sink and camping toilet. Yuck.

Then, there were the reliability considerations. Light plane piston engines aren't designed to run that long without maintenance, so the team developed a special lubrication system, allowing the oil and filter to be changed while the engine droned on. Sounds a bit dangerous.

As for fuel, the standard wing tanks holding about 50 gallons weren't going to cut it. They'll only run for 5 or 6 hours before going dry. Timm added a belly tank, adding an extra 95 gallons, which could be pumped into the standard fuel tank system as needed during the flight. This modification reduced the need for refueling to twice per day.

THE FLOOR IS LAVA

The whole point of a record endurance flight is that the plane can't land—ever—for gas or anything else. The team found an abandoned desert highway for creative ground-to-air refueling. A truck on the ground would match speed and direction with the low-flying plane, which lowered a hook to grab a fuel line and whatever supplies were needed, like food and water. While driving and flying in formation, with the plane about 20 feet off the deck, goods were transferred by hose and rope twice a day for 65 days in a row.

To make sure there were no secret "quick landings," shortly after the fight took off on December 4th, 1958, the plane made a low pass, matching speed with another truck, whose brave crew member reached up and painted the plane's wheels white. The idea was that before the final landing, the record judge would inspect the tires to ensure there were no scuff marks from secret landings.

AFTERMATH: THE LONGEST FLIGHT EVER

It took three failed attempts, the longest being 17 days, to get the kinks out, but on the fourth try, success. Almost 65 days, 128 truck-to-plane refuelings, and 150,000 miles of brain-rattling low-speed air travel later, the endurance record was shattered.

By that time, the team only had to beat 50 days (another attempt was made in parallel, barely breaking the previous record), but they elected to remain in the air as long as possible in hopes of discouraging any others crazy enough to try to knock them out of the record books.

Needless to say, it wasn't easy. The generator system broke not long after the halfway mark, meaning all fuel pumping had to be done by hand and flying without lights inside or out at night. Ponder a night refueling exercise using the team's truck-to-plane method. Worse yet, not being able to stretch out or stand for over two months left the pilots incapacitated by the finish—they had to be lifted out of the plane after landing.

But the record still stands to this day. If you want to see the plane, just look up when in the Las Vegas Harry Reid Airport Baggage Claim area—it's hanging on display.

PART III
CULTURE

In show business, the key word is honesty. And once you've learned to fake that, you're in.

George Burns

Personally, I'm always ready to learn, although I do not always like to be taught.

Winston Churchill

Learn the rules like a pro, so you can break them like an artist.

Pablo Picasso

A man can never have too much red wine, too many books, or too much ammunition.

Rudyard Kipling

FRANKLY, I DON'T GIVE A DAMN

Spoken by apathetics and those wishing to appear so everywhere, the "I don't give a damn" barb has got to be one of the most used and abused argument finales ever. Who doesn't know this one? The year: 1939. The line spoken by Rhett Butler (Clark Gable) to Scarlett O'Hara (Vivien Leigh) in 1939's classic blockbuster, *Gone With the Wind*, was, "Frankly, my dear, I don't give a damn."

DAMN, IT'S FAMOUS!

In 2005, the famous quote was voted the number-one movie line of all time by the American Film Institute. Interestingly, that list's number two movie quote was, "I'm gonna make him an offer he can't refuse." That line was delivered by Marlon Brando, who wasn't a fan of how Gable dropped the verbal apathy on Scarlett. Apparently, Brando didn't care for Gable's too-slow and dramatic walk to the door in that scene. I guess he thought the lead-up to the delivery of the iconic line was a bit too contrived.

DAMN, IT'S SCANDALOUS!

Arguably, Rhett's "damn" line ushered in a new era of profanity in the movies. While the word had been used in a handful of silent films and talkies before *Gone With the Wind,* the movie industry censors had started to crack down on potty mouth words since the 1930 Motion Picture Production Code. Also known as the Hays Code, the rules were part of an industry-wide self-censorship initiative.

Although rumor persists that *Gone With the Wind* producer David O. Selznick was fined $5,000 for using "damn" in the film, it seems more likely the script was approved as part of a production code amendment allowing the use of "hell" and "damn" when the words were essential to the portrayal of the story or taken from a literary work, etc., etc. As it turns out, the original text of Margaret Mitchell's novel of the same name used the phrase, "My dear, I don't give a damn." Close enough.

DAMN, IT'S... WHAT IS IT, ANYWAY?

For something so commonly used in spats everywhere, have you ever wondered why we say this in the first place? Like most traditions, there are a couple of competing theories.

The word "dam" (no 'n' in the original Middle English version) has been around for a long time, say back to the 12th to 16th centuries, at which time it wasn't necessarily considered profane. The verb meant something like "to condemn" or "to declare guilty."

It was derived from the Latin word "damnare," also meaning "to doom" or "declare guilty." Add the religious angle of damnation or condemnation to hell, and the meaning has remained somewhat constant over the centuries. Some etymologists believe that over the years, folks started to use the phrase "don't give a damn" synonymously with "I don't care."

But there's a far more fun and interesting possibility. Like most things, I suspect these dual paths melded at some point, as a good play on words is always a crowd-pleaser.

In the 18th century, British troops arriving home from India reportedly brought the phrase back to jolly old England. The Indian "dam" was a coin of near worthless value, at least compared to the pound sterling. Accordingly, it's easy to see how one might express a condescending attitude about not giving a "dam" for, well, whatever. Add in the play on words factor, shifting "dam" to "damn," and we have a winner.

THAT OTHER ONE...

Wherever Rhett Butler's speechwriter stole the phrase, at least it's been preserved more or less intact over the years.

That other big one, you know, "Play it again, Sam," has been edited over the years into something that never actually happened. The famous line from *Casablanca,* uttered by Rick (Humphrey Bogart) in most misquotes, was actually, "Play it." But even that's a little misleading, as similar lines are delivered by both Ilsa (Ingrid Bergman) and Rick. When Ilsa walks into Rick's bar and sees his long-suffering piano player, she sits down and says, "Play it, Sam. Play *As Time Goes By.*" A little later, proving he can handle the painful memories from the couple's past fling in Paris, Rick makes a similar request.

Oh, and in case you're wondering, Ilsa's version of the famous line lands at number 28 on the AFI movie quote list.

WHY DO WEEKS HAVE SEVEN DAYS?

Sometimes, time divisions just make sense. For example, a day is intuitively defined as the duration from when your snooze button refuses to work until the nightly Chicago police/fire/medical/cosmetology disaster TV show wraps up another episode. Of course, some people consider a "day" as the time it takes for the Earth to rotate once around its axis. Whatever.

There are other sensible divisions of time. The Earth orbits the sun once a year—every 365 days. Well, to get picky and offer up another trivia tidbit, it takes 365.25 days. That quarter day adds up, and if you do the simple math, it becomes apparent why there's an extra day in leap years every fourth year.

So, there's rhyme and reason to the year concept, too.

MOONTHS

No, that's not a typo. Months also have some logic backing their existence.

There are 12 lunar cycles during the Earth's 365-day trip around the sun. Well, technically, a lunar cycle of all the phases is 29.5 days. Just in case you've heard a figure of 27 days, 7 hours, and 43 minutes, that's how long it takes for the moon to orbit the earth. In either case, we're in the reasonable ballpark of a "monthly" correlation. We just have to forgive the rounding errors—astrophysics is complex stuff; just ask Carl Sagan. Apparently, somewhere along the line, someone forgot to carry the one.

As the legend says, even the term "month" derives its name from the moon. If we lived in a true democracy, I'd vote they ought to be called "moonths," but the powers-to-be have more pressing things to worry about, like making shady land deals for personal enrichment. See the Politics section in this book for stories about that.

WHAT A DIFFERENCE A DAY MAKES

So what about weeks? Why is a week seven days long? Why is this division roughly a quarter of a month or a fifty-second of a year? If you compare a week to a true lunar month, it works out to 23.728 percent of that. It adheres to no apparent logic, offends my sensibilities, and the metric system is likely apoplectic over the sheer disorganization of the whole weekly concept.

BORN IN BABYLONIA... MOVED TO ARIZONA

While it wasn't King Tut (Sorry, Steve Martin, it would have made a great lyrical addition to your song), it was King Sargon I of Akkad who helped introduce the seven-day week. He is ancient and most likely dead by now, having ruled around 2,300 B.C.

In that time and place, the number 7 held special significance. It's also the number of major celestial bodies that can easily be seen by the naked eye: the sun, the moon, Jupiter, Mercury, Saturn, Mars and Venus. Remember, the Hubble Telescope didn't go into service until April 25, 1990, one day after its launch. Well, its performance was limited at first due to a glitch in the mirror, but that's a story covered elsewhere in this book.

The Jews also favored a seven-day week. There's the book of Genesis in the Bible, which outlines the concept of a seven-day time scale for creation, including the seventh day of rest.

Of course, weeks are kind of arbitrary, and one can ask why we even have them at all. But people were enamored with the idea, even though, in the absence of a celestial calibration with orbiting bodies, they created "weeks" in their own likeness anyway. The Romans ran with an eight-day week. The Egyptians favored a 10-day week. Hard workers, those Egyptians.

So why did the magic number seven win out? The Jews were held captive by the Babylonians during the peak of Babylonian influence, and both cultures favored the concept of seven days for different spiritual reasons. The Persians and Greeks followed, then Alexander the Great, and we all know how much influence he had.

Eventually, even Rome shaved a day, and now we all live a septenary life.

THE LEFT LANE IS FOR PASSING ^&%$#(@!!!

So, can you or can you not take legally justified umbrage at Sunday drivers puttering along in the left lane as if it were their personal cruising track? Few driving practices create more road rage and, in my opinion, accidents. Car and Driver magazine agrees, "A 2016 AAA study found that nearly 80% of drivers reported feelings of anger and aggression when slow drivers wouldn't get out of the left lane, and 51% said they 'purposefully tailgated.'"

While not a federal law but rather a model act created by a non-profit organization, the Uniform Vehicle Code states, "Upon all roadways, any vehicle proceeding at less than the normal speed of traffic at the time and place and under the conditions then existing shall be driven in the right-hand lane then available for traffic ..." Translation: the left lane is for passing.

It's not binding, of course, but it's pretty clear you're supposed to get the heck out of the left lane if you're idling along. And many states back up this suggestion with law. The specifics vary.

DON'T MESS WITH ... THE LAW

While every state claims to have the worst drivers, I can definitively state South Carolina has the highest per-capita number of left-lane cruisers, especially on the stretch of I-26 between Charleston and Columbia. I have it on good authority (because science) that people from all over the country who believe their tax dollars entitle them to drive 45 mph in the left lane move here for the express purpose of driving back and forth between South Carolina's two largest cities. #Fact.

Little do they know they are breaking the law. In 2014, two fed-up state reps sponsored a "get your slow butt out of the left lane" law, making driving in the left lane illegal. It's now for passing only. Tell that to the snowbirds. While there are some reasonable exceptions, like when no one else is around, or traffic is heavy, violating the law under normal circumstances will get you two points on your record.

Other states take a similar approach. While we can't cover all 50 here (look yours up to be safe), many including Massachusetts, Pennsylvania, Minnesota, New Jersey and others, driving in the left lane for no reason and not yielding to traffic wishing to pass is illegal. That applies even if the left lane putzer is a "Karen" wishing to forcibly impose the speed limit on everyone else because of their inherent righteousness and compulsion to virtue signal.

Other states have reserved all other lanes except the right one for passing. In Missouri, Maine, Montana, New Jersey, and Washington, the center lanes are reserved for passing, too, unless you have a good reason for being there, like an upcoming left turn or exit. Sadly, I have yet to witness someone getting pulled over for clogging up traffic in this manner. I think we can all agree that's a national tragedy.

California does not necessarily agree. Rob Lund, a California Highway Patrol spokesperson, referred to the "left pane is for passing" controversy as a historical carryover, stating, "It goes back to when the roadways were, at best, two lanes in each direction, and it was kind of an unwritten rule that the left lane was for passing." Trailers and such are discouraged, and you can be cited for driving too slow in the left lane, however.

You might hear a reference to the "Hammer Lane." That is believed to be a carryover from trucker lingo, also referring to the passing lane. As you might have guessed, it's derived from "hammering" the accelerator to speed up and pass slower traffic.

SO, WHAT TO DO?

Details vary by state, but in many places, it's acceptable etiquette to use your left blinker or a high-beam flash to indicate to a left-lane hog you want to pass. In no states, except apparently South Carolina, is it legal to ride the person's bumper until they move. Yes, that's the leading cause of accidents when everyone is going in the same direction.

To beat this dead 1986 Lincoln Continental just a bit more, if nothing else, do your part to improve road manners. Be aware. If there are 15 cars lined up behind you in the left lane, just keep diddling with your phone and ignore all those hacked-off drivers. Or, perhaps, consider moving over. Remember this mantra: slow lane ... go lane.

If you want to lobby your state legislature to put some teeth behind the complaints, take a hint from a successful Ohio road sign campaign, "Camp in our state parks, not in the left lane."

ABOUT THAT NEW YEAR'S EVE TIMES SQUARE BALL DROP

We've devised many weird ways to celebrate the instant the clock turns 12 on New Year's Eve. I've been to a flip-flop drop, a giant blue crab drop, and a few other small-town Americana versions of the traditional New Year's Eve celebration. Of course, the one that gets all the TV coverage is the Times Square Ball Drop in New York City, where they de-elevate a giant crystal ball filled with lights to mark the precise moment a new year begins. Before we get into the fun stuff, let's be real. There's no dropping going on here; it's more like lowering with extreme care. That party decoration is expensive, valued at over $1 million.

DROP IT LIKE IT'S WEIRD

The Times Square giant Waterford Crystal Ball is pretty tame when you start looking at some of the other things we drop in various parts of the country. Some items pair, as you might expect, with the local culture. Memphis drops a giant guitar, Nashville drops a giant Musical note, and Atlanta, Georgia drops a giant peach. Considering the city has 71 streets with variants of the Peachtree name, no one is surprised by the peach theme.

Boise, Idaho, drops a giant potato, while Orlando goes with their stereotypical orange. Miami adds a bit of style using a giant orange wearing sunglasses. Must be a South Beach orange.

From here, things start to get weird.

Mobile, Alabama, uses a giant Moon Pie.

Lebanon, Pennsylvania drops bologna. Yes, really. No word on whether the bologna has a first name.

Las Cruces, New Mexico, likes to keep things spicy and goes with the ever-popular chili pepper.

Eastport, Maine, drops a giant sardine.

When you stop to contemplate the possibilities, you won't be surprised that Key West, Florida, takes the prize. Multiple drops throughout the town include a giant conch and a SMART car-sized high-heeled red shoe, complete with a drag queen inside for the ride down. To top things off, the Schooner Wharf Bar organizes the lowering of a pirate wench.

ABOUT THE TIMES SQUARE BALL DROP

All this dropping has been going on for a long time. While the partying tradition began years earlier, the first big ball fell in New

York in 1907. Made from iron and wood, it was powered with festive 25-watt lights. Those are less powerful than the ones in your oven. Hey, electricity hadn't been around all that long, so I'm still impressed, especially with its five-foot diameter and 700-pound weight.

Over the years, ball designers made logistics easier with lighter balls. In 1920, the ball went all iron, which you might think would be heavier, but it only tipped the scales at "just" 400 pounds. In the mid-50s, aluminum replaced iron, and the ball slimmed down to a cool buck fifty.

For the 2000 celebration, Waterford Crystal and Philips Lighting collaborated on a complete redesign, going with something much closer to today's sparkly design. In 2007, the 100th anniversary of the New York Ball Drop, the companies came up with a doozy, leading to the "permanent" (or permanent until the next redesign) of the ball we use today.

THE MODERN NEW YEARS BALL

What you saw in the last moments of 2023 and the first moments of 2024 was a genuine whopper. The Waterford and Philips ball is 12 feet in diameter and weighs just shy of six tons at 11,875 pounds.

There are 2,688 Waterford Crystal triangles defining the surface. They're comprised of different sizes and designs. Upon close inspection, you'll see crystal designs symbolizing various "gifts," including, but not limited to, love, happiness, goodwill, wonder, serenity, harmony, and more.

Under those crystals are 32,256 LED lights with equal numbers of red, blue, green, and white. Those lights can create an overall color palette of over 16 million shades.

THE ORIGIN OF BALLS

This isn't all frivolity, you know. Back in the day, many port cities used prodigious dropping balls to publicly communicate a point in time so ships could calibrate their onboard clocks. Knowing the precise time was essential to their ability to calculate longitude. Without that, sailors were, by definition, lost at sea the moment they ventured past the sight of land. There's a great book about that, by the way, *Longitude*. It's a highly recommended read.

WHY DO WE TELL PERFORMERS TO BREAK A LEG?

It sounds like bad juju, but theater people are a unique breed. It takes ~~illimitable insanity~~ guts and perseverance to stand up in front of hundreds or thousands seven or eight times per week and sing and dance your heart out.

And then there are the critics. Being a live performance art, there's little room to hide behind a product, service or company. It's no surprise why the community has historically embraced a bit of superstition and rituals to combat disaster. But "break a leg?" Why is that the universal wish for good luck? Why is saying "good luck" really bad luck?

I'm gonna warn you now. There is no definitive answer as to the origin of "break a leg" because whoever started it didn't take the time to file a copyright claim. But at least all of the theories make for an interesting story. Let me know which one you find most credible to you, and we'll settle on that...

Before we start, I should mention there is fairly solid agreement the practice started around the 1930s, so take the timeline into consideration when choosing your explanation.

THERE IS SUPERSTITION

Since I brought it up, we might as well cover the obvious one first.

There are all sorts of theater superstitions ranging from "don't say 'Macbeth' in the theater, else you'll curse the show!" to the last person to leave turning on a "ghost light" in the middle of the stage. In a nod to the lamp superstition, Steve Martin, Martin Short, and Selena Gomez worked that one into their series, "Only Murders in the Building." While we're at it, one shouldn't whistle on the premises either.

Above all, never say... "Good Luck!" A superstitious mind believes saying "good luck" is asking for bad luck, and saying something tragic, like "break a leg," really calls for good luck.

Meh. There are more compelling possible origins; let's move on.

LANGUAGE MANGLING

If you've got your Yiddish and German pronunciation nailed, you might buy into one of the more popular theories for the origin of "break a leg."

A Hebrew maxim of "hatzlakha u-brakha" translates into something like "success and blessing." When pronounced correctly, it sounds something like a German saying, "Hals-und Beinbruch." That translates into "neck and leg break," which is admittedly not very funny on its own apart from the identical-sounding Yiddish blessing.

We love our puns. This theory might make cents if you're a betting person.

BOWS AND CURTSIES

A truly vainglorious bow requires participation from the body complete. One leg goes back, the other bends deeply, and arms flourish to the sides. One might consider that a form of "breaking" a leg.

A BANGIN' GOOD SHOW!

After Ancient Greek performances, audiences showed their appreciation of a particularly good performance by stomping their feet. Later, in Elizabethan times, rabid theater fans would smack their chairs on the floor for the same reason. "We were at the theater when a professional wrestling match broke out!"

Whether real or chair legs, the idea is you're wishing a performer to do so well that the audience breaks "legs" at the end of the show.

PRESIDENTIAL ASSASSINATION?

In the interest of being thorough, I have to bring this up, but it's admittedly difficult to believe this story inspired the official birth of the "break a leg" phrase.

John Wilkes Booth was a somewhat popular actor before killing President Lincoln. After he fired the shot, mortally wounding the President, he jumped from the President's box down to the stage, promptly breaking his leg.

How this scenario was believed to become a good luck wish escapes me.

CURTAINS FOR YOU...

There's a "line" on the stage defined by vertical curtains along the sides of the stage. Their purpose is to block the view of off-stage actors, production folks and set items from the audience.

One school of thought assigns the "break a leg" origin to performers who may or may not make it past that "leg line" and onto the stage. In olden days, if you weren't on stage, you didn't get paid. I suppose that's the ultimate commission plan—perform or don't collect a check.

So, "breaking" the leg line was a wish to get in the game and collect a paycheck, so to speak.

Other related stories describe "breaking a leg" as coming through two center-stage curtains for an encore. If you "broke" those curtains, you were enjoying encore applause, presumably after a stellar performance.

BACKSTABBING UNDERSTUDIES?

Someone has to say it, so I will...

Has anyone questioned the understudies? It's not out of the realm of possibility they might wish for the lead to "break their leg" (but not too badly, right?) so they can get some stage time themselves.

Always a bridesmaid and never a bride.

HOW KISSING UNDER THE MISTLETOE CAME TO BE

Why do we kiss under the mistletoe? Sure, teenagers have been snogging in the bushes for eons. And who hasn't stolen a buss (a very old school word for 'kiss') in front of the Christmas tree?

KJÆRLIGHETENS GUDER (GODS OF LOVE)

While the Druid and Celtic cultures have associated mistletoe with fertility thanks to its evergreen qualities, the Nordic peoples might have started the osculation ball rolling. Word has it the Norse god Balder was killed by an arrow made of mistletoe. When his mother Frigg cried over him, her tears turned to white mistletoe berries. She declared the berry tears a symbol of love and promised to kiss anyone passing beneath it.

A VICTORIAN HALL PASS

Before and during the Victorian era, someone, perhaps a brilliant and amorous British male, developed a social custom where any young lady standing under the mistletoe could have a smooch planted as long as berries remained. When the berries were gone, the lass was off the market for more kisses.

FAKE MISTLETOE

Mistletoe's evergreen qualities are part of the reason for its fertility and romance associations. The fake stuff, which comprises the majority of what we see, has the green part right, but where it "kinda" drops the ball is that most faux-toe features bright red berries. However, the traditional version of European mistletoe (Viscum album) has white berries. There is a newer natural variant with red berries, the American Phoradendron.

TRUE LOVE POISONED

What does mistletoe have in common with cashew nuts? I knew you were just dying to know, so here goes.

As discussed elsewhere in this book, raw cashew nuts share a family lineage with poison ivy. That's why they're always roasted and not available in stores raw. Mistletoe berries are also poisonous, a strange attribute for a plant associated with kissing! Lower dose exposure causes digestive distress, while more can impact heart and lung function. Don't freshen your breath with the berries before planting one on your mistletoe partner!

Now freshen up with a Wint-o-green breath mint and let the sparks fly!

WHY IT'S OK TO BURY THE HATCHET, JUST NOT IN SOMEONE...

I've been watching a creepy series on Netflix recently... *You.* It won't be much of a spoiler if I say that sometime during the series, a certain someone buries a hatchet in a certain someone else's back. The "bury the hatchet" recipient kind of had it coming, but even still, it was somewhat of an impulsive display of overreaction.

This whole episode got me thinking... While "bury the hatchet" is a common phrase we use today, it certainly is an odd way to describe forgiveness and reconciliation unless, by reconciliation, you mean hacking your enemies into mincemeat.

A FEARSOME WEAPON

The "hatchet," better known as a tomahawk, was a serious club-like weapon with an edge. Dating back to stone-age times when a sharpened rock would be attached to a sturdy handle, the weapon has been a symbolic and literal harbinger of war and conflict for centuries.

The tomahawk has enjoyed a modern resurrection due to its utility as both a tool and a weapon, making it popular among even modern warriors. Back in the mid-1960s, a World War II Marine Corps vet, Peter Lagana, reimagined the tomahawk and built versions that became popular with troops in the Vietnam War. Now, it's not unusual to find modern warriors still using them. For what it's worth, the lead character of former Navy Seal Jack Carr's popular *Terminal List* hero puts one to gory use. We'll leave it at that in case you haven't yet read the entire series.

The modern tomahawk is quite a handy tool, especially in the woods.

BURY THE HATCHET ORIGIN STORY

The practice of burying weapons of war (the tomahawk in this case) dates back to a Native American practice of warring tribes to come to a peace agreement by quite literally burying a symbolic tomahawk as a promise it would no longer be wielded in anger. Presumably, should relations decay, the weapon would be dug up, symbolizing a declaration of war.

Iroquois legend credits one notable origin theory to two visionary Native Americans, Dekanawidah and Hiawatha, who saw the wisdom in advancing the cause of peace and civil society among tribes back in the late 16th century. The Iroquois Confederacy was originally formed by the alliance of the Mohawk, Oneida, Onondaga, Cayuga, and Seneca. In a far more tradition-laden and binding ceremony than signing a piece of worthless paper, chiefs from each nation buried their weapons under the roots of a large pine tree, from which an underground river washed them away, never to be used against each other again. In theory.

LITERAL HATCHET FUNERALS

While idioms like this one are largely passed through generations verbally, "bury the hatchet" has been used quite formally on numerous occasions.

In Article 11 of the Treaty of Hopewell, which in 1795 established the boundaries of the Cherokee Nation, we find the following reference, "The hatchet shall be forever buried, and the peace given by the United States, and friendship re-established between the said states on the one part, and all the Cherokees on the other shall be universal; and the contracting parties shall use their utmost endeavors to maintain the peace given as aforesaid, and friendship re-established."

During what we might loosely refer to as the Pilgrim era, Samuel Sewall wrote in 1680, "of the Mischief the Mohawks did; which occasioned Major Pynchon's going to Albany, where meeting with the Sachem they came to an agreement and buried two axes in the ground; one for English another for themselves; which ceremony to them is more significant and binding than all Articles of Peace the hatchet being a principal weapon with them."

Now, if we could only find a way to bury cable news programming…

CONFUSING ABBREVIATIONS, E.G., "ETC." AND "I.E."

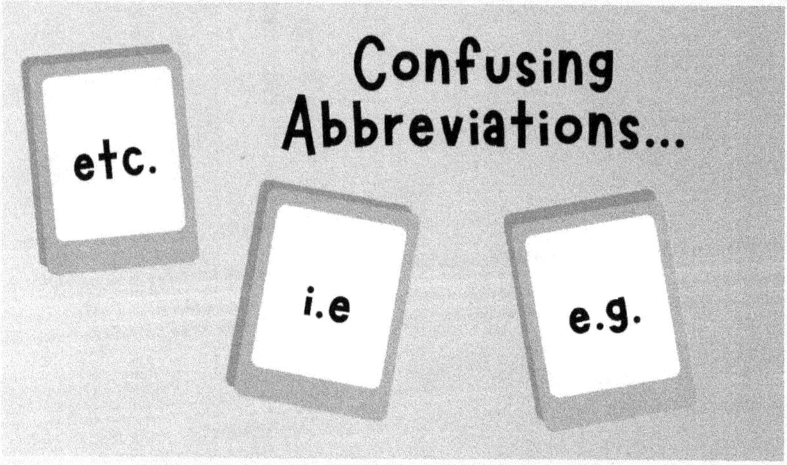

Can grammar be practical? Sure, if its inadvertent misuse causes readers to raise their eyebrows and wonder about the writer's credibility. Think resumes, work communications, etc. See what I did there? We're getting into today's topic already! Three abbreviations seem to get abused more than others, e.g., "etc.," "i.e.," and, you guessed it, "e.g." See what I did there???

The good news is proper use is easy when you know the origins. Let's go!

ETC.

Abbreviated from the whole word, etcetera, or in older times, et cetera, this one has been around quite a while, perhaps earlier than the 15th century. Charles Dickens used it frequently, one example coming from *The Pickwick Papers*.

"At the upper end of the room was a table, with a white cloth upon it, well covered with a roast fowl, bacon, ale, and et ceteras."

When you break down the full word, etcetera, its meaning and proper usage become much less confusing. The original Latin, two-word phrase, et cetera, translates as follows. Et means "and," while cetera implies "the other parts" or "that which remains."

So, simply put, etcetera can be used to communicate "and all the other parts" as in a list of similar things.

I.E.

This one derives from the Latin "id est." That means something like "that is." Think of "i.e." as an introduction to a clarifying statement or possibly an alternate way to express an idea. The simple shortcut to proper use is mentally substituting the phrase "in other words." If your usage still works, you're good to go.

When pondering whether you used this one correctly, try substituting a different phrase, i.e., words with similar meaning, to test the success of your sentence.

E.G.

Let's go to the Latin first, and all will become clear! "E.g." stems from "exempli gratia," meaning "for example."

So, when communicating an idea and you want to provide examples to clarify or reinforce the precise meaning, use "e.g."

To add interest to your written ideas, try using a vocabulary reference, e.g., a thesaurus, to find alternate word choices.

THE BOTTOM LINE

To refine the quality of your writing, engage your readers, etc., try using abbreviations, i.e., shortened forms of words. You know, like those Latin abbreviations, e.g., "i.e." and "etc."

ABOUT THOSE NEW YEAR'S RESOLUTIONS...

Every year, millions of us discard New Year's resolutions like those tuna fish casserole leftovers from a week ago Thursday. In fact, only about nine percent of people who set New Year goals ever come close to completing them. By the end of week one in January, about one-fourth of resolvers bail on their resolution plans. By the end of the first month, another quarter fall by the wayside. If you're keeping track, that's a 50 percent attrition rate by January 31.

That's almost as bad as the failure rate among med school wanna-be's once they hit the collegiate organic chemistry weed-out class.

WHY THE SAD FACE?

Researchers have examined the colossal surge of optimism and good intentions that ring in every new year to figure out why more people fail at completing New Year's resolutions than wash out of the indoctrination Navy SEAL BUD/S (Basic Underwater Demolition / SEAL) course. Figures vary a bit, and the Navy doesn't go out of its way to publish the exact numbers, but approximately 80% of supremely in-shape humans don't make it through the 24-week training program, much less the entire six-month grueling process just to become a "rookie" SEAL, at which point the real learning starts.

As for resolution failure rates, about one-third of resolvers wash out because they say their goals were too unrealistic from the start. Another third fails to keep track of their progress, and you know what they say about proper goals needing to be measurable. A quarter of those with great intentions just plain forget to follow through, and another small segment makes too many resolutions to manage.

A (HOPEFULLY SUCCESSFUL) NEW YEAR'S RESOLUTION IN ACTION

I have an ego-shattering confession. I earn my living writing pithy stuff and... I can't type. To clarify, my fingers fly over the keyboard, but an observer would likely ask if I'm related by blood to Edward Scissorhands.

I've never counted, but I'd guess 60 percent of strikes are made with my index fingers and the leftovers are handled by the middle fingers. Are you supposed to use the ring and pinky fingers while typing? Over the years, I've become passably adept, if spastic, with my home-grown Mavis Beacon horror flick method, and I usually don't have to look at the keys. But I know it's a bastardization of basic humanity.

What offends my soul is my long-suffering tolerance to the concept of productivity. My brain wants to output far faster than my fumbled fingers can handle, so let's just say my daily endeavors could be improved immensely with proper typing skills.

TYPING SPEED AND ACCURACY

I've never done this until just this moment, but I found an online typing speed test and gave it a whirl. My words-per-minute typing speed worked out to 58 with close to a ten percent error rate—and that's after autocorrect fixed most of my typing mistakes on the fly. Without that, I'd have a 20 percent (or more) mistake ratio. Ouch.

While the speed isn't completely embarrassing (40 wpm is the average for a true, ten-finger, touch typist), becoming "fast" would require getting into the 80 or 90-wpm range and reducing the mistakes—a lot. Even those fixed by autocorrect are distracting to the composition process.

It's time for a New Year's Resolution.

SMART GOAL SETTING

To avoid the washout resolver crowd, I need to be SMART about this. Rather than just saying, "My New Year's Resolution is to get better at typing," I need to break it down using the SMART goal-setting and achievement method.

Specific: I want to learn how to properly touch type with all ten fingers so I can be more efficient in my work. It will be hard to overcome decades of bad habits.

Measurable: I want my speed to average 80 wpm and my error rate to be less than five percent.

Achievable: I know I can do this because my job allows (forces) me to practice for many hours a day. The world's fastest typists exceed 200 words per minute, so if I can't reach just 80, with all my practice, I'm lame.

Relevant: Typing literally feeds my family. The more efficient I am at putting my thoughts on paper, the more likely I am to continue having a roof over my head and food on the table.

Time Bound: My time allotted is one year. Of course, any improvement along the way will be a bonus.

THE 10-MINUTE MARATHON

I figure breaking this down into daily tasks will facilitate the process rather than just hoping my "goal" will work itself out by the end of a year. I see a two-part challenge.

First, I've got to learn exactly how to use all ten fingers the correct way so I can break my hunt-and-peck habit and devote all my daily writing to practicing correctly.

I acquired a simple app that offers daily practice drills to train your fingers and brain to touch type the right way. I figure if I repeat each lesson two days in a row, I should be able to cover the entire keyboard (slowly) by the end of February. This step is the key. My focus needs to be on completing a 10-minute learning session for about 50 days in a row. I can do that.

Second, once I have enough muscle memory to know where the keys are for each finger, I can officially transition all my actual writing to the proper method. I figure I'll be as slow as a congressman reaching for the dinner check and have plenty of errors, so the next part of the plan will involve forcing myself to accept the productivity loss while I build speed with the new and proper method.

The plan will both get me transitioned and give me ten months of daily "practice" (while I'm working) to build speed. A quick online test monthly will track my progress.

I'll know next January how it worked out. Got resolutions of your own? Try the S.M.A.R.T. plan.

THIS STORY IS NOT ABOUT THE ORIGIN OF "RED HERRING"

Do you know what would be genuinely mischievous? To write an article, purportedly on the origin of the phrase "red herring" and then steer the reader off the cliff into an 800-word abyss on some other topic altogether... See what I did there?

"That's just a red herring" is something we see in social media spats daily. Good mystery novels will have subtle red herrings to steer the reader's brain in the wrong direction, thereby setting up the shocking "I didn't see that coming!" ending. Nations have even left misleading clues to turn the tides of a World at War. Like, oh, say, planting a dead guy in the ocean, dressed as a high-ranking officer, with a briefcase full of fake invasion plans. Perhaps dead men do tell tales, but that's another story.

So why do we talk about "red herrings" when referring to intentional (or unintentional) misdirection?

WHAT'S A RED HERRING?

Just so we're all on the same page, besides being a fish, a "red herring" in this context is a clue that misleads from the correct conclusion. Simply put, it's a false clue or at least a distracting one that sends the clue solver's brain in a different direction. Think distraction from the main issue.

Before we get too far into this, it would be responsible to note red herrings (the fish) do not exist in nature like Red Snapper or Red Drum (Redfish.) They're a man-made concoction from regular, run-of-the-mill, non-red herring. When subjected to the smoke and salting process, herring can turn bright red (and become even more stinky.)

If you're a conspiracy theorist, you might even think the name "red herring" is a "red herring" in itself, as there is no such fish...

EXAMPLES

Politicians use red herrings all the time. To avoid getting sued, I'll make up a not-very-unrealistic scenario...

> Press: "Did you attend a Tupperware Party with that woman who is not your wife?"

> Politician: "That's a great question, and I am happy to answer it. This is precisely why I've always voted for post offices to be named after famous pet Chihuahuas."

I think the producers at Dateline use red herrings regularly. By showing an interview scene early in the show, taking place in an ambiguous room that *could* conceivably be somewhere in a prison, they misdirect the viewers on who might really be responsible for that episode's murder.

As for literary use, read most any Sherlock Holmes story, and you'll get your fill of red herrings.

FISHY DOGS AND FOXES

Long before the invention of station wagons and minivans, when people rode horses a lot more, fish was used to train hunting dogs to follow a scent, leading the horsemen along the desired trail. With its not-insignificant smell, dragging dead fish around the farm to create a scent trail was a way to give untrained hounds an easy path to follow. Then again, a stegosaurus with allergies could follow a scent like that.

As with many of these things, there is some disagreement about when the first usage occurred. The Farmers' Almanac folks claim the first use in print dates back to the year 1686 when a writer suggested dragging a dead cat, or if that was unavailable, some red herring around the area to prolong the thrill of a fox hunt.

While fish, and particularly pungent red herrings, were used to train dogs, there is not much evidence they were used as distractions until a story written by William Cobbett in 1807. In that fictional piece throwing shade on the English press at the time, he described using red herring to distract the dogs from a real hunt from the scent of a hare.

We know virtual red herrings work as they're used all the time. But can actual red herrings create enough confusion to mislead tracking dogs so central to this tidbit of history? As it turns out, the team at Mythbusters did an episode on it. After the dog found and ate the red herring, it backtracked and reacquired the correct scent trail.

PART IV
SPORTS AND RECREATION

Sport does not build character, it reveals it.
John Wooden

Talent wins games, but teamwork and intelligence win championships.
Michael Jordan

You miss 100% of the shots you don't take.
Wayne Gretzky

WHO PAINTED THAT YELLOW FIRST DOWN LINE ON THE FOOTBALL FIELD?

Ever wonder about that yellow first-down line we see on the football field during broadcasts?

Because we love a good conspiracy, there are plenty of folks who remain convinced the lines are added with powerful lasers or disappearing paint. I'm not sure about that paint theory... do sports ball gnomes run out on the field between plays to repaint the lines?

As it turns out, the reality is not far from the fantasy—it's a pretty impressive technological undertaking, shared with your local TV meteorologist, to make those lines we take for granted appear under your favorite player's shoes.

CANUCK ROOTS

After a shot-down proposal in the late 1970s, part of the inspiration came from hockey, when in 1996, FOX introduced a nifty glowing puck graphic overlay on that tiny little hunk of rubber so easily lost amid the chaos of grown men fighting on ice.

Infrared transmitters were embedded inside the puck, which communicated with sensors scattered around the outside of the rink. This allowed the system to follow the puck by creating a blue glow around it. When the puck speed exceeded 70 miles per hour, the effect changed to a red comet streak. Think dramatic shots on goal resembling epic *Star Wars* battle scenes.

Fan reviews were mixed on "glow puck," and the effect was retired a few years later. But entrepreneurs are nothing if not persistent, so the engineers at FOX Sports who came up with this stuff left and founded their own company—SportVision, Inc.

MAKE A NEW PLAN, STAN

Future National Inventors Hall of Fame inductee Stan Honey founded SportVision in 1998. Prior to going solo, Honey worked at News Corporation (owner of FOX Sports, among other things), where he helped launch broadcast innovations like the glow puck.

While rookie players were fighting through 1998 pre-season games to earn roster spots, SportVision was testing and furiously fine-tuning a new system they hoped to sell to ESPN for NFL game broadcasts. Parked in a separate truck next to the ESPN command trailer, the team sent a test feed complete with the new first down yellow line.

During the last pre-season game in Kansas City, the system worked pretty well, with only a bit of line jitter. After a couple more weeks in the lab, the system was ready for its public launch during a regular season game between the Baltimore Ravens and the Cincinnati Bengals on September 27, 1998.

A few weeks later, former collaborator but now rival company Princeton Video Image launched its version of a virtual first down line in a Steelers-Lions game televised by CBS.

THE MAGIC… EXPOSED

Step one in the process is for the tech gurus to create a digital map of each field prior to the game using sophisticated laser technology. Remember, dudes paint the lines on the field by hand, and who knows if they're a bit hungover. Also, remember that each field is curved to different degrees depending on the local climate—the center from goal to goal is higher than at the sidelines to allow for drainage.

Once the computer has a virtual map, it can begin the business of trying to calibrate cameras with constantly moving action on the field. Not only are the players moving, but through pan, tilt, and zoom, the camera image is also in non-stop motion. This is just the beginning of a hairy technological process.

The system not only needs to know the precise location of each camera around the field, but each needs to be equipped with sensors to monitor and transmit pan, tilt and zoom information to the system. The cameras need to be calibrated with each other to determine which is providing the current live feed.

And it gets even harder. Camera lenses introduce a bit of distortion to the picture, so while the white lines actually painted on the field are straight, the image on your TV screen has a bit of curvature. So, the technology has to introduce just the right amount of imperfection to the yellow line, too, or else it would look different than the lines painted on the field.

You won't be surprised to know a mathematician was part of the original development team.

UNIFORM CONFLICT RESOLUTION

A more subtle feature of "make or break" importance is making sure that the yellow line appears painted on the grass at all times. When a player runs or falls across that line, it must be "drawn," so it's underneath them as if it were painted on the blades of grass or astroturf.

That takes some doing and is the part borrowed from your local TV affiliate's weather team. For each game, the shades of green (and maybe brown, depending on the grass condition) are sampled and programmed into the computers—leveraging the chroma-keying "green screen" process. Then, the players' uniform colors are sampled and factored in.

Once the computer understands the color shades of the field (and remember, it has to account for things like passing clouds and rain or snow), it can work on the gargantuan math problem of figuring out where to add yellow in each frame of live video. Don't forget that cameras are moving throughout all of this, so the position of each pixel of the first down line must be re-calculated relentlessly. All of this work is done with less than a one-second delay from real-time action.

BIG MOVES

So there you have it. We'd be remiss not to mention Jed Drake, head of Event Production at ESPN at the time. For this to get off the ground, the SportVision team needed a sales commitment. Seeing the potential but not knowing how fans would react to artificial elements being introduced to the raw view of live sports, he took the plunge and signed a one-year exclusive contract on behalf of ESPN. The rest is history.

If you're watching football this season, thank the engineers at SportVision and Princeton Video Image, but don't forget to give a nod to your local weatherperson.

THE PERFECT MARCH MADNESS BRACKET: LONG ODDS

Each spring, all the basketball fans and those with gambling in their blood talk breathlessly and relentlessly about the perfect March Madness bracket.

The program includes 64 college basketball teams duking it out in a single-elimination tournament to figure out who takes the title. The "bracket" is a chart of all 63 matchups that cascades the winner of the first round into succeeding round matchups.

Technically, 68 teams start if you count the "First Four" games, but most brackets only include the ultimate 64 teams. In the end, two teams remain and play for the championship.

The real fun, besides watching some great basketball, is pondering the odds of picking a perfect March Madness bracket—choosing in advance the outcome of every one of the 63 matchups. As we'll see, the odds of success are, well, astronomical, which explains why no one has yet succeeded, and it's a safe bet to say no one ever will.

PERFECT MARCH MADNESS BRACKET ODDS MATH

We're gonna keep the math simple, but as you'll see, the numbers get really big, really fast. Each game has two outcomes, so if we assume we're choosing the outcome of each game by a random coin toss, kind of like playing roulette, we determine the odds of success by using simple exponents—two to the n-th power, where "n" equals the number of contests.

Keeping with the standard bracket design, there are 63 games, each having two possible outcomes. So the odds are 2 to the 63rd power. The resulting number will melt your calculator.

9,223,372,036,854,775,808

Got that? I'll translate it for you. It's 9.2 quintillion.

Just for kicks, if you were to expand the bracket to all 68 initial teams, your odds of perfection work out to...

147,573,952,589,676,412,928

That's 147 quintillion.

WHAT'S A QUINTILLION?

A quintillion is a lot—more than Congress can spend on ridiculous things in a six-year Senatorial cycle. Put into more digestible terms, a quintillion is one billion billion.

Ask any Swifty worth their Spotify playlist, and they'll tell you Taylor Swift is worth about 1.1 billion dollars, but let's call it an even billion. Now imagine she lays out each of her dollars in a line. Now imagine the recording industry clones another 999,999,999 Taylors, and they do the same. So we have one quintillion dollars all lined up end to end.

That line of dollar bills would be 6.14 quintillion inches long, or about 96,800,000,000,000,000 miles. Given that a light year represents only about 5,880,000,000,000 miles, we're figuring it would take 16,486.49 years, traveling at the speed of light, to zoom by those one quintillion dollar bills lined up so neatly. Heck, we could get to the nearest star with planets in just 4.24 light years, so we're talking really large numbers.

QUINTILLIONS SANDS IN THE HOURGLASS

Sticking with our random bracket-picking strategy for a standard bracket and the one-in-9.2 quintillion chance of getting it all right, we can bring the visualization a little closer to home.

Some geologist slash mathematician with way too much time on his hands tried to estimate how many grains of sand exist on planet Earth. We'll spare you the method and say it was an estimate based on the total volume of sand on the coasts, under the sea, and elsewhere, with some ballpark math counting how many grains of sand are in a cubic yard of the stuff. The result? About 7.5 quintillion grains of sand.

So, if I choose one specific grain of sand somewhere on planet Earth and ask you to guess which one it was, the odds of you getting it right are about the same as picking a perfect March Madness bracket. Yeah, I know, we're about 1.7 quintillion off, but what's a billion billion or two among friends?

PERFECT MARCH MADNESS BRACKET GURUS

Thus far, we've been assuming you're randomly guessing at the outcome of all the bracket matchups. In reality, lots of sports fans out there have some knowledge of the teams involved and can make more educated guesses about who is more likely to win specific games. This knowledge increases your odds of a perfect March Madness bracket—a lot.

While subjective, many agree that history and statistics can do a pretty good job of picking winners in advance. To put a number on the success rate, the "knowledge" strategy works about 75% of the time. That means 25% of the matchups, give or take, are unpredictable upsets.

ODDS OF SPORTS FANS' PERFECT BRACKETS

If you subscribe to the intelligent picks model and have to account for a 25% upset rate, your odds improve to somewhere between 1 in 10 billion and 1 in 50 billion.

Let's split the difference and say we're looking at a 1 in 30 billion chance of success. While not guaranteed because random chance is, well, random, you might say we have a reasonably good chance of someone getting this right if we run 30 billion March Madness Tournament bracket selections. That's 30 billion years if just one person plays. By then, a semester of college will cost a quintillion dollars, so those basketball scholarships will be sought after big time. If more people participate and choose brackets, you can do that math.

WARREN BUFFETT BELIEVES

Warren Buffett is the sixth richest person in the world (depending on the day), yet he's known for his shockingly frugal lifestyle. He still lives in a house he bought for $31,500 back in 1958. He still drives a 2014 Cadillac XTS and has been known to purchase cars with slight damage and cosmetic blemishes to save a few bucks. The point is, he's loathe to part with a dime.

Yet he's so convinced of the practical impossibility of picking the perfect bracket that he's put up big money over the years for the person who can get it right.

Back in 2014, Buffett offered a $1 billion prize to any Berkshire Hathaway employee who picked a perfect bracket. Later, he amended the program to $1 million yearly for life and added lower-level prizes for coming close.

Sorry, employees only, so if you're feeling lucky, apply for a job there. Just don't start spending your winnings in advance.

LOVE-15! WHY IS TENNIS SCORING SO WEIRD?

While tennis isn't exactly one of those weird sports (it's impressively athletic), it does have the most bizarre concept of score. I have it on good authority the Gatorade jugs on the court are spiked with LSD. It's the only logical explanation of tennis scoring.

NO ONE LOVES A ZERO

Well, some do. Darts players covet the big goose egg when playing 301, as the objective is to subtract scores until one lands precisely at zero, but other than that, most sports reward larger scoring numbers. A zero generally means you're losing and wasting perfectly good oxygen.

Apparently, tennis players care about hurting opponents' feelings, as there is no zero in the game. To avoid the emotional trauma of being temporarily shut out, they've invented a new, kinder, gentler term to communicate to players and observers alike that you've accomplished nothing thus far in the game. But don't worry; everyone still has positive and affirming feelings for you.

LOVE MEANS YOU STINK

In relationships, love means never having to say you're sorry. In tennis, love means your opponent isn't sorry at all. They want you to have all the love for the whole match. That's because "love" is another way of saying zero. Here's the proof in indisputable form: a dad joke.

Q: Why should you never fall in love with tennis players?

A: Because to them, love means nothing.

You're welcome. Use that on your kids if you haven't earned a good eye roll in a while. One day, after years of learning to cope with embarrassment, they'll one day remember the moment fondly.

EN FRANÇAIS

There is one possible French origin of using "love" to designate zero in tennis.

Although I did flunk 7th-grade French (really), I still remember how to say "egg." It's "oeuf." Take that, Mr. Morgan! In practice, you'd use the masculine definite article "le" before the "oeuf," but since the French word for egg starts with a vowel, you write it "l'oeuf."

While I don't think "oeuf" and "love" sound much alike, enough people do believe this is the origin of saying "love" to indicate zero in tennis. An "egg," or, more often, "goose egg," often is used to communicate zero, and "oeuf" sounds a bit like "love," so people just started calling zero points "love."

It's a weak theory in my book; most people believe the true origin lies elsewhere.

IT'S JUST A GAME

A more likely origin story of "love" in tennis derives from the game's civilized nature. For example, the Wimbledon tournament has been going on for nearly 150 years. During all that time, the organizers have maintained a strict all-white uniform policy, down to players' underwear. Yes, really. It wasn't until 2022 that the All England Club allowed women to wear dark underwear underneath white shorts or skirts, provided the shorts or skirt were longer. Why white? Early sport elders didn't want to tarnish the genteel image of the game, with players' clothing showing sweat stains. Apparently, it was considered poor form for athletes to perspire during play.

As a refined sport appreciated by high society, it might have been considered low-brow for players to compete primarily for the purpose of winning or (gasp!) earning a victor's purse. Civilized athletes should play purely for the love of the game, with all after-effects being considered a fringe benefit not to be gloated over. And there you have the most popular origin theory of "love" equating to a score of zero.

Even though you've failed to score points, your "love" of the game keeps you on the court faithfully representing the noble sport of tennis.

WHY IS A FOOTBALL QUARTERBACK CALLED A QUARTERBACK?

The reason behind naming quarterbacks "quarterbacks" isn't exactly what we'd call a profound mystery. As one might guess, the name did, in fact, have more than a little to do with the player's starting position relative to the line of scrimmage. In the early iterations of the game, with the standard offensive formation, the quarterback was halfway between the holder of the ball (center) and halfback. The halfback was halfway between the center and the fullback.

RUGBY ROOTS OF THE QUARTERBACK

In this case, however, there's a lot more to the story, and that's where the fun facts lie. The quarterback's position (and naming) was closely intertwined with the development of American Football. Notice I didn't say "invention" of football. The sport we know today is an evolutionary offshoot of the rough-and-tumble game of rugby from across the pond.

Central to the story is one Walter Camp, a naturally gifted athlete and Yale student. Learning a new game (to him) called rugby, Camp became involved in negotiations and rule discussions between the athlete powers-to-be at a number of Ivy League schools, including Yale, Harvard, Columbia, Princeton and the like.

During the 1870s, rugby matches were decided by the number of successful "goals" following "touchdowns." To make a long story short, many felt touchdowns should carry much more weight in the score outcome (see the future here?), and Harvard, Princeton and Columbia formed the Intercollegiate Football Association. Others soon joined.

FOOTBALL PLAYS ORIGINS

Re-enter Mr. Camp. Fed up with the chaotic start of play from a classic rugby scrum, Camp advocated for a more orderly strategy by each team to better prepare and execute planned tactics. Sound like today's plays?

Camp wrote the following proposed rule, "A scrimmage takes place when the holder of the ball puts it on the ground before him and puts it in play while on-side either by kicking the ball or by snapping it back with his foot." Yes, you read that right. The early centers "snapped" the ball into play using only their foot to… the quarterback. Clever centers learned to tap the ball with a foot to start play, then pick it up to hand off to the quarterback. One thing led to another, and before long, quarterbacks took snaps directly from the center.

NOT VERY QUARTERBACK-LIKE

Things were a little bit different in the early days of quarterbacks...

Quarterbacks were frequently lead blockers for halfbacks and fullbacks. Apparently, in the days before nine-figure contracts, quarterbacks were considered expendable.

Initially, the quarterback could not advance the ball beyond the line of scrimmage. In fact, it was a big no-no. Per Walter Camp, "The man who first receives the ball from the snap-back shall be called the quarter-back and shall not rush forward with the ball under penalty of foul." As a side note, the hyphen in "quarterback" was lost over the years, saving valuable ink and now electrons.

The quarterback was also prohibited from throwing the ball downfield?!? It was downright "illegal" until 1906.

Although quarterbacks assumed the role of captains and play-callers, football remained a strongly "running against the defense" type of game, with half or fewer of all plays involving a forward pass (a 3:2 run-to-pass ratio in 1977, for example) until 1978, when a significant rule change (no contact with receivers past five yards from the line of scrimmage) changed everything. Now the big bucks go to the guys with big arms who can toss laser beams downfield with abandon.

Oh, and you won't see them blocking very often.

DODGEBALL OR DEATHBALL? THE REAL ORIGIN OF THE GAME

What possessed us to invent a game, presumably one for kids, where the object is to fling a ball at an opponent with enough force to prevent them from catching it? As I remember the rules, nothing is sacred. Leg, body, extremity, and full-on facial shots are all "American Dodgeball Association... Of America" approved. (Warning: There may be plenty of *Dodgeball* movie references in this piece. Deal with it.)

Sensitive area strikes were a sure way to put all players on the floor laughing hysterically. Then again, our proclivity for violent contact in sports isn't unique to dodgeball. Football, hockey, and even baseball reward the big hits. Baseball? Yes. It is the baserunner's sworn duty to steamroll a catcher threatening to force an out-at-home plate. If you hit him hard enough, he'll drop the ball, and you'll be called safe while the fans cheer your manliness.

In the movie *Dodgeball: A True Underdog Story*, Patches O'Houlihan (the younger version played by Hank Azaria) explains the origin of the game to young Timmy in an educational film. "You're in a Chinese Opium Den, Timmy. This is where the sport of Dodgeball was invented in the 15th Century... by Opium-addictive Chinamen. But back then, the Chinamen threw severed heads at each other instead of the A.D.A.A.-approved balls we use today."

Yes, the movie was a comedy, but this depiction of the origin of the game isn't all that far off the mark…

WAR PREPARATION

Designing activities and sports aimed at prepping a population for future wars isn't anything new. Humans have been doing that for 75 percent of forever. Read *Gates of Fire* for an account of the Spartan Agoge culture, a structured way of life and training to turn young Spartan boys into citizens… and warriors. In the book, young Xeones describes activities such as groups of boys marching relentlessly, shields pressed against an immovable tree, to build strength, persistence, pain tolerance, and esprit de corps. Sounds fun, but I preferred skateboarding in the street.

Back to dodgeball.

ROCK ON!

As it turns out, the fictional Patches O'Houlihan is a fountain of real-life wisdom. In the movie, he pontificates, "Dodgeball is a sport of violence, exclusion, and degradation." And if you look at the history of the sport, not to mention the modern-day jocks destroying the bookworms version, it's not far off the mark. Historically, dodgeball likely was a way to weed out the weaker of the tribe.

Most dodgeballologists believe the sport originated in Africa a couple of hundred years ago. Like the Spartans, tribes developed ways to build toughness, strength and team (tribe) cohesiveness as a way to prepare for war. If some of the weaker participants got killed in the process, well, that's just a way to ensure the ranks are filled with nothing but the strongest fighters. Elite military units still do this, but usually without the death. Those who aren't in the toughest tier simply quit or are otherwise washed out.

So, what's this talk about "death" from dodgeball? The original form of the activity used large rocks instead of rubber balls. The goal was to incapacitate opponents, knocking them silly to the ground, at which point the "pile on" of more hurled stones began. The "defending" team would rally to protect and recover their wounded counterpart. If a few got killed in the process, that was the cost of realistic battle training.

DODGEBALL MISSIONARY

One Dr. James Carlisle, a missionary working in Africa, saw the "sport" firsthand and figured it was a healthy physical and team-building activity—if one left out the whole "mortal combat" part. He brought it back to England and organized a kinder and gentler version using rubber balls instead of stones while teaching at St. Mary's College. Killing off students in PE class is often frowned upon, even at the collegiate level.

AMERICAN DODGEBALL ASSOCIATION... OF AMERICA!

Well, the movie got one thing right, but they did change the name to protect to protect the virtuous. The ruling authority on real dodgeball competitions is the World Dodgeball Association. They're legit and facilitate sanctioned competitions around the world. Do be aware there is a serious anti-doping policy, just like in the movie. So, no anabolic steroids or low-grade beaver tranquilizers are allowed.

WHY DO TENNIS PLAYERS GRUNT?

There's a whole lot of grunting going on here. I'm catching a couple of first-round matches at the Credit One Charleston Open WTA 500 event. While not the biggest women's tennis tournament on the tour, it's got a million-dollar prize package, and the conditions are glorious—Charleston, SC, in the spring couldn't be nicer.

While watching the first-round play between Danielle Collins and

Paula Badosa, I couldn't help but wonder why so many tennis players grunt when they strike the ball. Danielle and Paula let the screams and groans fly consistently, as did most other players throughout the day. As if tennis wasn't unusual enough with the scoring, now we have to explore the reasons behind animalistic rituals.

TENNIS PLAYERS GRUNT FOR RELAXATION

It's no secret that top athletes play at their peak when their bodies and minds are relaxed. When their mind is Zen, and they're not focused on the outcome, but instead on the moment, they perform at a higher level. That's a difficult state to achieve when the stakes and pressures are high, hence the reason leading sports psychologists get paid the big bucks. Just ask any top professional athlete to show you those canceled checks.

A power grunt forces air out of the body, potentially releasing muscle tension. Some players report that their primal exhalations help keep them on an even "stress level" during a match.

MIND GAMES?

Watch any Hollywood action hero flick and there's inevitably a scene where the good guy is in serious trouble, but he uses a mind game to throw his opponent for a loop, thereby creating an opportunity to turn the tables.

Obviously, grunts can be distracting, but they can also mask the sound of one's opponent's strike on the ball. After hitting a few million balls in practice, a top player gets cues as to velocity and direction from the sound of impact. Without that input, some studies have measured slower reaction times by the defender.

TENNIS PLAYERS GRUNT FOR MORE POWER

Probably for a variety of reasons, players are able to hit with measurably more authority when grunting. Combine some relaxation and stress relief with a focus on the moment of impact, and that grunt can make your serve or return even faster.

Studies have demonstrated that grunters can increase the power of a groundstroke by up to four percent, and the benefit is even more substantial when serving, nearing a five percent increase. When you stop to consider the minuscule performance differences between winning and losing at the top tiers of the sport, a few percentage points might just be the difference between going home empty-handed and millions in prize money plus a wall of major tournament trophies.

PREDICTIVE TENNIS GRUNTING?

Here's a fun angle on grunting science you can put to the test the next time you watch a match.

Like other mammals on our planet, grunts' tone and sound can mean a lot. Generally speaking, a lower-pitch grunt (or roar in the animal kingdom) is a sign of dominance or, in our sporting world, victory. Higher-pitch grunts are often observed with less dominant behavior or, in sports, frustration and loss.

If you hear your favorite player's grunts increasing in pitch, maybe prepare for a tough loss.

All that grunting must be exhausting. From informal observation of the Danielle Collins vs. Paula Badosa 1st round match, while the grunting on both sides was powerful and consistent in the first set, it ebbed and flowed during the second. Alas, Collins maintained the lower-pitch grunts, winning 6-1, 6-4.

WHY DO BASEBALL PITCHERS WARM UP IN THE BULLPEN?

Watch any Major League or College Baseball game, and you'll hear the word "bullpen" a couple dozen times. We don't bat an eye about it now, but if you stop and think, it's kind of a weird word to describe the waiting room for pitchers hoping to see some game time. Like other odd sports terminology, for example, the word "quarterback" in football, there's a story behind the name.

So, what's the origin of the bullpen?

MAYBE MAD MEN INVENTED THE BULLPEN

Ads have been plastered around baseball field fences since horse-drawn wagons roamed the earth. One theory of the origin of the term "bullpen" assigns the name to ads sponsored by the Bull Durham Tobacco Company.

As you might guess, an ever-present icon of the company's brand was a large bull. So, if you imagine big signs plastered along the fences, players would be warming up "under the bull."

While this idea has some merit, there is evidence the term "bull-pen" was used long before relief pitchers became a regular part of the game in the 1890s.

An additional bit of trivia: you'll notice "bullpen" is both hyphenated and not in this story. That's intentional as the use of the term evolved over the years.

BULLPENS: THE CHEAP SEATS

If you build it, they will come, even if they can't afford regular seats.

There used to be a happy middle ground between pricey reserved seats in the stadium and the iconic knothole in the outfield fence. Areas called "bull-pens" in outfield foul territory were reserved for the really cheap seats, where impoverished fans, or those with less disposable income, were packed in like cattle. Some stadiums even allowed these bovine spectators to drift into the stadium after the first inning or so.

Over time, as stadiums expanded by adding bleachers and the foul ball territory area, bullpens became the area where relief pitchers warmed up—close to the action but still out of the field of play.

FROM THE HISTORIAN'S MOUTH

Last but certainly not least, as the purveyor of the final theory has impeccable street creds, is the idea that the term came from a mid-19th century game called... bull-pen.

As Major League Baseball historian John Thorn describes, the game, popular in the midwest around the 1850s, involved two teams of players, one of which surrounded an area called the "bull-pen." The opposing team was inside, and the contest somehow involved throwing a ball. Ipso facto e. pluribus unum, the relief pitchers' enclosed area is still called a "bullpen" to this day.

Of course, this explanation isn't mutually exclusive with the foul territory cheap seats idea, as when relief pitchers came into vogue, they often warmed up in the same areas previously occupied by rabid fans low on funds. So, in all likelihood, since the term "bull-pen" was associated with baseball in general terms in the 1870s and with relief pitcher warm-up areas around the turn of the century, the origin of today's bullpen was somewhat evolutionary.

WHAT EXACTLY IS "PLAY ACTION" IN FOOTBALL?

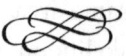

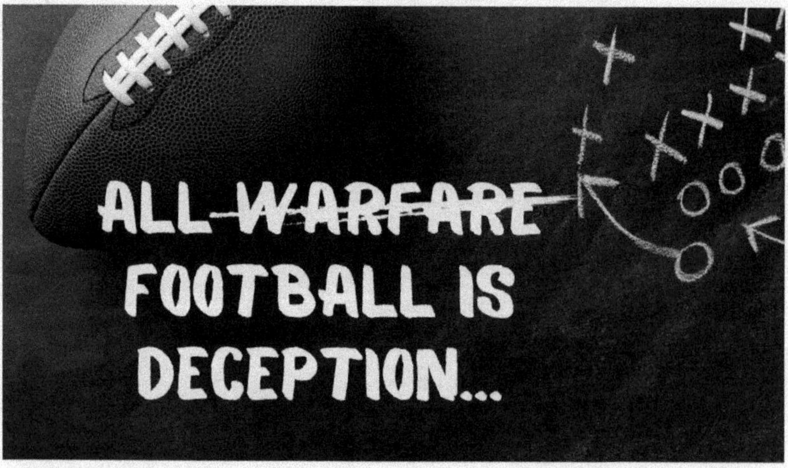

Watch any football game, and you'll hear the term "play action" more than anything else, except perhaps the word "scamper." I'm all for free speech, but can we all agree on just one exception? The word "scamper" should be banned from use by any football commentator. Thank you.

So, back to the topic at hand, what is "play action?" It sounds like it could accurately describe any football play. "Playing" and "action" happen every time the ball is snapped, right?

OK, if this is one of those terms you heard so often, for so many years, you're embarrassed to ask its meaning, never fear. We're going to cover it here, and you can pretend you knew it all along—we won't tell.

PIGSKIN YIN AND YANG

To fully understand the utility of the "play action" pass, it's good to know its polar opposite—the draw play.

The draw is a running play that appears to be a pass play. The receivers take off downfield to draw defensive backs into deeper pass coverage. The linemen go into pass protection mode but, at the same time, encourage the defensive line to move to the outside. "Sir, would you kindly rush the passer from the outside rather than through the center of the line?" The quarterback drops back as if to pass. Last but not least, the running back hangs out in the backfield as if to block pass rushers, giving the quarterback more time to find a receiver and complete a pass.

If all goes to plan, there's now a gap in the center of the line, usually the "A-gap" between the center and guard, and the defenders ideally cleared out, the quarterback hands off to the running back, who has some space for a big gain. A variation on the play—the quarterback draw—has the QB fake the pass, then tuck the ball and run himself.

PLAY ACTION: FOOTBALL FAKERY

A "play action" play is the other half of the opposing pair of play designs in the repertoire of strategies designed to fake out the defense. In short, it's a play designed to look like a run but really is a slow(er)-developing pass play.

The neat thing, if you watch a perfectly executed "play action" play, is the calibrated symphony of cooperation by the entire offense to sell the scam. Linemen blast forward as if to clear a path for the sans-ball runner—before falling back to provide pass protection for the quarterback. Receivers come off the line, blocking linebackers and secondary defenders—before breaking loose to run a pass route. The quarterback fakes a handoff to the running back, who steamrolls through the line, taking whatever punishment is awaiting, even though he doesn't have the ball. And last but not least, the quarterback, after faking that handoff, casually looks for an open receiver. In a perfect scenario, one or more receivers are open downfield as pass defenders have relaxed coverage to defend a run.

With the defense now committed to defending a run, the quarterback completes a big pass, wins the game and humbly accepts eternal glory and a generous contract extension.

WARFARE IS DECEPTION

As military strategist Sun Tzu said in *The Art of War,* "All warfare is based on deception. Therefore, when capable, feign incapacity; when active, inactivity. When near, make it appear that you are far away; when far away, that you are to lure him; feign disorder and strike him. When he concentrates, prepare against him; where he is strong, avoid him."

Works for football, too.

PART V
SCIENCE, TECHNOLOGY AND NATURE

Somewhere, something incredible is waiting to be known.
Carl Sagan

We are stuck with technology when what we really want is just stuff that works.
Douglas Adams

Look deep into nature, and then you will understand everything better.
Albert Einstein

SCHRODINGER'S CAT: THE PRACTICAL GUIDE TO RADIOACTIVE FELINES

If you dislike cats, you'll love Schrodinger's Cat. I guarantee it.

You see, Schrodinger's cat is locked inside of a sealed box. Inside the box is a radioactive element, a Geiger counter, and either some poison or perhaps some type of explosive. Schrodinger was a twisted thought scientist because he deigned to rig this setup in such a way that when (or if) the radioactive element decayed at some random time, it would trigger the Geiger counter, which would, in turn, release the poison or launch the feline-seeking Hellfire missile.

Before you get too upset with Schrodinger, know this whole thing was a concocted story to be used as a teaching aid, arguably to put physicists he disagreed with to shame, ideally making them realize their theories were preposterous. Or not. Because quantum physics is really weird stuff, and no one agrees on much of anything.

QUANTUM PHYSICS OBSCURA

So, without going completely off the rails (Practical Guides promise practical knowledge and brevity), part of quantum theory claims that particles can exist in a superposition of states at the same time. Positive and negative. Hot and cold. Democrat and Republican. Only when interacting with other particles do they "collapse" into a single state.

So, to apply a digestible analogy, imagine you're a particle sitting on your couch, and simultaneously, you're both eating Brown Sugar & Cinnamon Pop-Tarts and not eating Brown Sugar & Cinnamon Pop-Tarts. It's only when your spouse enters the room, smacking you upside the head and asking why you're not mowing the lawn, that you collapse into a single state of either snacking or not snacking—but not both.

I know, even with the Pop-Tart analogy, this is heady stuff. That's why professional physicists have unkempt hair. They're too confused by their own theories to remember to comb. #Fact.

PHILOSOPHY AND OBSERVATION

Quite by accident, my Pop-Tarts analogy is kind of on target for the point of this whole cat story. You see, these superposition theories drift into the philosophical world, where observation causes the particle in a state of superposition to collapse to a single state. Or, in your case, it's the act of your spouse walking into the room and seeing what's going on that creates the single state of you either eating or not eating the Pop-Tart. If he or she hadn't walked in, you'd blissfully be both eating and not eating indefinitely. Physicists call this the observer's paradox. Wild huh?

ALIVE OR DEAD? WHY NOT BOTH?

Following this quantum logic, the cat in the box (remember, it's sealed, so none of us know what's really going on in there) could be alive or dead at any given nanosecond. Or, because quantum physics is crazy stuff, the cat is both alive and dead—a state of superposition in both meowing and non-meowing states.

As this thought experiment goes, it's the act of opening the box to see what's going on that causes the cat to collapse to a single state of either being perfectly alive or quite dead.

THE POINT OF SCHRODINGER'S CAT

Schrodinger was a smart guy, and I don't know if he disliked cats, but his "thought experiment" was not actually performed in a lab unless some overeager undergrad completely misinterpreted his lecture back in the 1930s. His purpose in concocting this scenario was to point out his belief in the fallacy of the observer causing the collapse of a particle from a superposition state to a single state.

Of course, nothing is ever simple, so while a superposition-state cat, both dead and alive, is beyond our comprehension, the behavior does seem to happen with certain subatomic particles. The gotcha is what causes the collapse into a single state. That's an argument for a new day, and lots of very smart quantum physicists have lots of diverse opinions on the matter.

As a sneak preview, one school of thought leads us to the "many worlds interpretation," which essentially states the universe splits into two diverging worlds upon opening the cat box, one where the cat is alive and the other where the cat is dead. Imagine that happening every time you're eating Pop-Tarts.

WHY ARE THERE HOLES IN ELECTRICAL PLUGS?

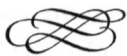

Here's one you see every single day of your life. But did you ever wonder why there are (almost) always holes in electrical plug prongs? Creatively presented, this bit of everyday practical knowledge just might win you a bar bet.

Let's solve this with a pop quiz.

Are the holes there to…

. . .

A. Save materials to reduce manufacturing costs?

Nope. While all that excess metal could, in theory, be recycled and converted into more plugs, it's not the answer. Besides, I'll bet Dunkin Donuts holds a patent on the productive use of what used to be holes. Besides, if this were the case, why not make the holes more oblong to save even more money?

B. The holes are there to catch on a spring-like device inside the plug to make it harder for the plug to slip out of the socket.

Again, nope. But there is just a hint of truth to this one. Back in the early part of the 20th century, there were a couple of patents floating around for plug prongs with notches in them. The interiors of receptacles would be equipped with springlike blades that fit into the "U-shaped" notches. To our eternal disappointment, modern plugs don't use any of that, and nothing inside the receptacles locks into the plug's round holes.

C. The holes are for safety locks to prevent people (think kids) from plugging stuff in that shouldn't be plugged in. Or to "lock" plugs into outlets with some kind of bar inside that goes through the holes.

Nope, but again, with a hint of truth, as such locking devices do exist, but the holes were there long before locks came on the market.

D. Because it's always been that way.

Winner, winner chicken dinner, but with a caveat. The prevailing wisdom is that once upon a time, manufacturers of plug-like stuff used the holes for manufacturing convenience—to hold on to the prongs while the plug body was formed or some such thing. Over time, these holes worked their way into the ANSI standards and are now precisely documented in terms of diameter and placement on the prong. However (and here's the fun part), there is a footnote saying the holes are completely optional.

So there you have it. Modern electrical gear manufacturers make holes in plugs, possibly for no reason at all other than "it's always been that way."

If only that kind of persistence applied to the price of bone-in ribeyes.

THE INVENTION OF STEREO: TWO EARS, TWO SPEAKERS

Before music was "on every corner" via iPods, iPhones, and smartphones, "stereo" was in practical use a word to describe almost any form of music player. It's kind of like using "Coke" to describe virtually any bubbly, sugar-laden beverage. You know, like Xerox for copies and Kleenex for boogers. The invention of stereo was far more interesting than office equipment, so let's dive in.

The word itself comes from the Ancient Greek term stereós,

which means something like rigid, solid, or even three-dimensional. Hold that thought for a hot second because it kind of makes sense to describe what stereo is really all about.

OLD SOUND, NEW SOUND

Recorded music dates back to 1877 (at least in practical terms) to Thomas Edison's invention of the Cylinder Phonograph and Emile Berliner's patenting of the gramophone, which used flat disks.

At the time, Edison was looking for ways to capture and re-use information transmitted through the telegraph and telephone. A paper tape contraption was the idea behind "recording" a telegraph message, while to save audio, Edison experimented with paraffin paper and foil-wrapped steel cylinders. He figured connecting a diaphragm to an embossing needle would carry sound vibrations through the needle, creating textured grooves in the cylinders. A separate playback needle and diaphragm sent the groove patterns back through a playback diaphragm, and voila! His first test of recording "Mary had a little lamb..." worked.

After a few decades, the technology improved, and many homes had record players that performed the same basic functions as Edison's Cylinder Phonograph but with flat discs. For purposes of this story, playback occurred through one single speaker and all sounds were combined in one output stream, what we refer to as "mono" or "monaural" today.

NOT VERY SURROUND SOUND MOVIES...

The modern era of stereophonic sound, worshipped by hippies, Deadheads and audiophiles everywhere, actually began with the movies.

Alan Dower Blumlein was a sound engineer at EMI (Electric and Musical Industries), one of the largest record and music conglomerates around. The consummate inventor and tinkerer, Blumlein's brain was still burning coal even when out for a relaxing night at the movies with his bride. After one such outing in 1931, Blumlein expressed frustration at the sound experience of the "talkies."

With sound coming from a single speaker, a viewer might hear the leading man (on the left side of the picture) whispering sweet nothings to the leading lady while the sound came from a speaker to the viewer's right. This is an extreme example, but it illustrates the problem of monaural sound. However you place the speakers, the viewer or listener's brain won't be able to triangulate the location of the sound with what they see on the screen.

STEREO EAR AND EYE PROCESSING

Just as a pair of eyes, combined with some brain matter, can estimate distance by "seeing" an object from two slightly different angles, that same brain can reconcile the origination point of a sound by hearing it from two different locations—the right and left ears.

If a tree falls in the forest somewhere off to one's left, the sound waves reach the left ear just a fraction of a second before the same waves titillate the right eardrum. The brain, being smart, figures, "Hey, the sound is coming from a place closer to my left ear!" And our brains, even among those who watch the Kardashians, are sophisticated enough that we can detect gradients, so via differences in when the left and right ears detect sound, we can figure a sound is coming from the 10 o'clock or 1:30 direction. Voila! We've just described what audio engineers and folks who drop ten grand on a hi-fi system call a sound field.

Bottom line: in the real world, our brains can do a bang-up job of figuring out where each sound originates. Close your eyes while listening to a live orchestra, and you'll be able to point to the location of each instrument.

BLUMLEIN'S STEREO INNOVATIONS

While there were some crude "two-channel" initiatives dating back to the 1881 Paris Opera at the Paris Electrical Exposition, the beginning of modern stereo really began with a slew of patents from Alan Blumlein.

In his first batch, he came up with ideas we still use today, like circuitry to preserve directional sound, microphone use and placement for recording in stereo and the method we use to capture stereo recording information in vinyl record grooves. All in all, Blumlein came up with more than 100 patents related to stereo, surround sound and other sound-related technologies.

EMI did put the technology to use almost right away, recording "Jupiter Symphony" by Mozart at EMI Studios, later renamed Abbey Road Studios. The team led by Blumlein also created movies to refine the concept, solving Blumlein's complaint of sound not following the actors on screen. One prototype film showed moving trains, complete with sound following the engines across the screen.

DEATH TO MONO; LONG LIVE STEREO

Like many innovations in the marketplace, it took some work for the public to catch on and insist on stereo sound for recorded music and movies.

Disney tried in 1940 with the release of their groundbreaking movie *Fantasia*. "Fantasound" featured multi-track audio recording played back through multiple speakers at specially-equipped theaters to render a form of stereo experience. Theater investment was significant, so the idea didn't catch on.

It wasn't until the late 1950s that record companies started to release stereo recordings, using the same "two-track" record groove technology Blumlein pioneered. As most consumers had mono record players, the two types of records had to coexist in retail channels for a decade, give or take.

During this time, clever marketers resorted to all manner of cool gimmicks like retail demo setups playing "moving sound" for curious consumers. RCA Victor even produced the stereo record "Sounds in Space" to capitalize on the space race frenzy.

A TRAGIC END TO THE BEGINNING

When World War II broke out, EMI talent was recruited to aid the war effort. Blumlein was instrumental in the development of a new navigation and target mapping radar system, the A2S. So, Blumlein's talents weren't at all limited to audio entertainment. Tragically, the war effort claimed Blumlein's life—he was killed in June of 1942 in a Halifax bomber crash, which also destroyed the prototype A2S system.

The next time you break out the classic audio gear and listen to "Dark Side of the Moon" and marvel at how the "three-dimensional sound" moves around the room, remember that clever audio engineer from the 1930s—Alan Dower Blumlein.

ROGER, ROGER... (.-. --- --. . .-. .-. --- --. . .-.)

> We have clearance, Clarence...
> Roger, Roger! What's our vector, Victor?

It's a classic line from a classic movie. But have you ever wondered why people on radios say the word "Roger" when acknowledging a communication?

It seems odd when you think about it. Why not "OK," or "Sure, no problem," or even "Thanks for calling; I hear what you're saying and will act on it post haste..."

Well, it all goes back to the very beginning of radio technology. Actually, scratch that. It goes back to the "two cans connected by a string" pre-radio technology—the telegraph. While the telegraph did go wireless, thanks to Guglielmo Marconi after his lab experiments in 1895, the early versions were corded, like really old VCR remotes.

So, the bottom line. Samuel F.B. Morse invented the telegraph, which was capable of transmitting basic electrical signals in 1835. The technology couldn't handle anything so complex as voice, just pulses of varying duration, so three years later, Morse and associate Alfred Vail created a coding system to represent letters and numbers, what we now know as Morse code—a series of long and short pulses (dots and dashes).

The first iteration was English-centric and not able to handle characters with diacritic marks. So, a bit later, in 1851, with lots of input from European nations, the International Morse Code was invented.

All this background has a point, so let's get back to the "why Roger" discussion.

In the days of telegraphs, tired fingers from all that button pressing (and brief holding for dash representation) led to the development of lots of single-letter shortcuts. If the message recipient wanted to say "received," they would simply reply with the Morse code representation of the letter "R."

It was a big deal, as you can see from the Morse code for "received" compared to the code for the letter "R."

.-. . -.-. . .. ...- . -..

(RECEIVED)

.-.

(R)

Ipso, facto, e. pluribus unum, the letter "R" became widely used as the standard acknowledgment of "message received, I got it."

Enter radios and associated static, especially in chaotic conditions, oh, like... war. A phonetic alphabet was developed, and an audibly unambiguous word was used for each letter of the alphabet. Back in the day, the word for the letter "R" was "Roger."

Those of you paying attention might call foul on this and claim the proper word for "R" is "Romeo." You're right. It is. Now. But back before NATO revisions in 1957, we did, in fact, use "Roger."

Just for kicks, if we ever have to revert to International Morse Code (it was used in shipping until the early 1990s and quite a bit in World War II and the Korean and Vietnam wars), we'd code it like this:

.-. --- --. . .-.

(ROGER)

Of course, in the military, we often hear a slight variation of "Roger" with the acknowledgment "Roger that!" but that's a story for another day.

So, in one of the greatest movies of all time, *Airplane* (OK, that's my opinion—I don't have a long list of Academy Awards to back up the claim), Victor's use of the word "Roger" is really a nod to the late, great, Samuel Morse.

.. .-.. . .- .-. -. . -.. ... --- -- . - .... .. -. --. --..-- .. .... --- .--. . -.-- --- ..- -.. .. -.. - --- --- -.-.--

(I LEARNED SOMETHING, I HOPE YOU DID TOO!)

BRING YOUR UMBRELLAS; IT'S RAINING INSIDE

"The NASA Vehicle Assembly Building (VAB) at Kennedy Space Center on Merritt Island, Florida, is SO BIG it has its own weather systems! Clouds, rain, fog—you name it!

Sorry, no snow. It's Florida. That's the story that started circulating during the construction of the world's largest one-story building. Started in 1963, the 526-foot-tall behemoth was finished in 1966 to house the giant, 326-foot-tall Saturn V rockets that took men to the moon, or, if you're conspiracy-minded, not. There's a story on that too in this book.

The raison d'être of the Vehicle Assembly Building is to complete the final assembly of massive spacecraft before they're wheeled out to the pad on that giant creepy crawler. So, the inside needs to be big enough to house the whole shebang standing upright, with lots of room to spare above for cranes and future (perhaps taller) rockets. To put things in perspective, the Saturn V rocket is about 60 feet taller than the Statue of Liberty. Imagine having that piece of sculpture entirely indoors.

After the Apollo program ended, the VAB was used for Skylab and 135 Space Shuttle missions. Currently, it's back in service for the Space Launch System (SLS) rocket and Orion spacecraft for the Artemis program.

NASA VEHICLE ASSEMBLY BUILDING FUN FACTS

How big is it? Try ginormous. The average "story" in a building is about 10-14 feet, depending on building materials used and such. The first floor of the VAB is about 52 stories tall in the area NASA calls the high bay. And there are four high bays, so back in the glory days of Moon landings, multiple Saturn Vs could be assembled in the VAB concurrently.

There are multiple cranes inside to hoist spaceships into position. Two of them are capable of lifting 650,000 pounds each. No sweat lifting an entire space shuttle, which only weighs about 165,000 pounds empty. If you loaded to the limit, one of those cranes could lift 162 average automobiles or 120 Tesla Model Xs. Those batteries are heavy.

When finished, rockets need to get out to the launch pad, so the VAB has some of the biggest doors in existence—465 feet tall. The overlapping door panels take about 45 minutes to open or close, so I suppose one has to plan ahead when leaving for the night.

Holding all that expensive rocketry gear takes a lot of space, and the VAB is one of the largest interior spaces in the world by volume. The interior space measures 129,488,000 cubic feet. That's almost four Empire State Buildings worth of room inside. In more practical terms, you could fit 44,262,234,814 iPhones in there, or for you foodies, almost three billion corned beef sandwiches.

WEATHER? OR SOMETHING LESS?

When you're dealing with that much un-air-conditioned space, it's going to get a bit weird at times. Leave the wrong doors open and closed when there are high winds outside, and you might encourage dangerous wind-tunnel effects inside. No one wants billion-dollar rockets tipping over like a Miller Lite longneck, so NASA has developed limits, weather triggers and procedures to govern the status of various doors.

If you forget to turn on the AC during off-the-charts Florida heat and humidity conditions, you can facilitate what some might arguably define as "weather."

Hot, humid air inside the VAB will normally rise, and as it goes up and up and up, the moisture in that hot air can condense, creating condensation on stuff at the upper reaches. As that accumulates, the water can fall (drip, really) and voila! With a bit of exaggeration, some might call it rain.

But that assumes no one remembered to turn on the massive 10,000 tons of air conditioning in the building. NASA says the giant air handlers can circulate all the air in the facility in an hour. Given that A/C keeps the relative humidity inside low, that's another strike against the claim of clouds and rain inside.

LEAVE IT TO THE ROCKET SCIENTISTS...

To ruin your day. As it turns out, while there are lots of stories that have circulated for the past 60 years about the Vehicle Assembly Building being big enough to have its own weather systems, NASA says ... no.

> Contrary to popular stories circulated during construction, the VAB, which is mostly not air-conditioned, does not create its own weather —reports of indoor rain, clouds, or fog are myths.

Boo.

CAN SNAKES SMELL?

As much as I hate snakes, biology swears I have two things in common with them. First, we both have pathetic eyesight. Second, our sense of smell, through the nose, leaves much to be desired. Sure, I can smell bacon sizzling, but outside of that and nearby paper mills, neither Serpentidae nor I am gearing up to compete on an upcoming episode of *America's Got Olfactory Talent*.

So, let's get to the topic of the moment. Can snakes smell things in any meaningful way? If so, how? If I freshen up with some Tom Ford Hombré Leather, will every cottonmouth in the swamp, sorry, I mean scenic wetlands behind my house come slithering?

HE SMELLETH WITH FORKED TONGUE

Most, or maybe all (I'm not willing to get close enough to look), snakes have nostrils and a rudimentary sense of smell through similar equipment to ours. But, unlike dogs, detecting scents that way is not among their superpowers.

Snakes have a high olfactory gear known as the Jacobson's (or vomeronasal) organ. Residing above the roof of their mouth, this organ has access to the inside of their mice holes through two small holes in their palette. Here's where things get creepy.

You know how snakes flick their tongue, scaring the crap out of people with self-diagnosed ophidiophobia like me? That has a purpose—to collect molecules of scent-generating things. Yes, when you smell something foul, little pieces of it are going into your mouth and nose, but that's a story for another day.

Anyway, the tongue picks up some bits of smelly matter, and when the snake retracts it, the material makes its way to the Jacobson's organ through those two little holes in the roof of its mouth. The Jacobson's organ is much more finely tuned to detect scent. You might say snakes reach out and touch the surrounding air, getting an olfactory swab, then process the "smell" by rubbing it on the roof of their mouths. Kind of cool. Creepy but impressive.

STEREO SMELL-O-VISION

Let's add a unique biological twist. Just like our eyes and ears can detect stereo, snakes can smell in stereo, thereby getting a directional sense of where the odor is coming from. A snake's tongue is forked, and as you'll remember, two holes in the roof of its mouth lead to the Jacobson's organ. Just as our eyes and ears process differing input signals, snakes process stronger or weaker scents from each side.

Since snakes flick their tongue around once per second, their little snake brains do an impressive job of figuring out the precise direction of the source of a scent. That's how they catch nimble prey like small critters so effectively.

Put all this together, and snakes can do a bang-up job of tracking live buffet opportunities by smelling with their tongue.

HOW MICROWAVE OVENS WORK: DO THEY REALLY COOK FROM THE INSIDE?

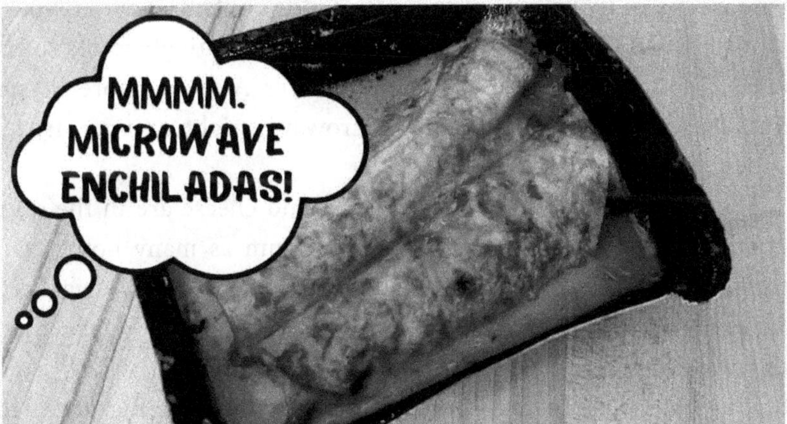

If microwave ovens heat food from the inside out, how come I always have cold spots in my spaghetti and meatball leftovers? And why is the cheese on top of my burger boiling while the center of my all-beef patty is just lukewarm? Well, microwave ovens are pretty darn convenient, but they don't perform sorcery. And they certainly don't cook food from the inside out.

MICROWAVES AND MAGNETRONS

A microwave oven is a pretty simple device when you get right down to it. It contains a high-voltage power source (driven by your wall outlet) and a magnetron, all packaged in a steel box acting like a Faraday cage to contain and reflect all those microwaves bouncing around and heating your food.

What's a magnetron? It's that thing Science Patrol member Shin Hayata used to hold up in the air to turn himself into *Ultraman*. Nah, just kidding, that thing was the Beta Capsule. According to the dictionary, a magnetron is an electron tube for amplifying or generating microwaves. Well, that's not very helpful, so let's try a different tack.

There's some complicated physics involved, but the components are fairly straightforward. A heated cathode beams out electrons toward an anode. But a powerful magnet redirects the path of all those electrons whizzing around. The anode contains cavities, which resonate when electrons fly by, but instead of creating audible sound waves like an oboe, they generate microwaves. A couple more physics tricks focus and aim outbound microwaves right at your frozen burrito.

The microwaves reheating your Mac and cheese are in the same general part of the radio frequency spectrum as many home electronics and networking devices. Remember all those 2.4 gigahertz marketing claims on slightly older wireless routers? Maybe that's why watching TikTok videos can get a little wonky when you're standing too close to the microwave oven while zapping your Hot Pockets.

HOW DOES YOUR FOOD GET HOT?

A standard oven definitely heats your food from the outside-in by using convection. A microwave also heats your food from the outside in, but in a different manner.

With a traditional oven, heating elements or gas flames generate heat, which warms the air inside the oven. The air surrounds your food, so heat is transferred to the surface of your dinner, eventually making its way to the middle of your pot roast.

You might have noticed the air in your microwave doesn't get very hot or even warm. That's because all those microwaves bouncing around inside aren't hot, at least in the traditional sense. What does happen is that the microwaves beam at your food, attacking it from the outside in—they don't magically find their way to the center of your frozen waffles, only to begin the heating work there. The microwaves beaming outside-in do get absorbed by certain substances like water, fats, liquid stuff in general and a few other substance types. As they get absorbed, water molecules (and similar, but we'll stick with water as it makes the best example) go berserk as they are bipolar in nature with positive and negative charges. They spin, dance and get excited, and in that process, emit a by-product of... heat.

So, in a sense, microwave cooking does kinda, sorta go directly to work on your food after passing right through most containers made of paper, cardboard, Tupperware and the like, but they certainly do not find their way into the center of your food first. Starting from outside-in, food is laden with excitable water and other molecules that generate heat in response to incoming microwaves. The more time your food is exposed to the bombardment, the deeper into the chicken pot pie the microwaves reach to continue the process, and the more opportunity the already hot parts of the food have to transmit heat around via convection.

WHY DO MICROWAVE OVENS SUCK AT CRISPY AND OTHER TIDBITS

When a conventional oven creates hot air to surround your upcoming meal, it evaporates water and applies direct heat to exterior layers. Like most anything organic exposed to heat, that creates a dry, crusty exterior. Mmmm. Brown food tastes good!

With no ambient heat, a microwave oven doesn't do much to create a scrumptious, flaky top to your pot pie. But food scientists have come up with somewhat of a lame solution. You might have encountered junk food designed and packaged for microwave cooking. Sometimes, especially for items with a crust, you'll get a cardboard package with a slightly metallic reflective surface. That's designed to heat up during the microwave process, hopefully generating a bit of evaporation and resulting crispy crust. Yeah, the food usually comes out soggy anyway. Conventional ovens have their place.

There's universal panic over putting metal in the microwave. It's not a particularly good idea, but not nearly as apocalyptic as the rumors suggest. That's because metal doesn't contain many excitable water molecules and reflects microwaves instead of absorbing them like your food. So, yes, some metal can create electrical arcs and damage your oven, but it's not likely to blow up the neighborhood. After all, the inside of your microwave is made of... metal.

One more thing. Don't worry about wearing lead overcoats while reheating leftovers with your microwave. The magnetron-generated radiation is non-ionizing, so it's nothing like the nasty stuff detected by Geiger counters.

MYTHBUSTING SILENCERS

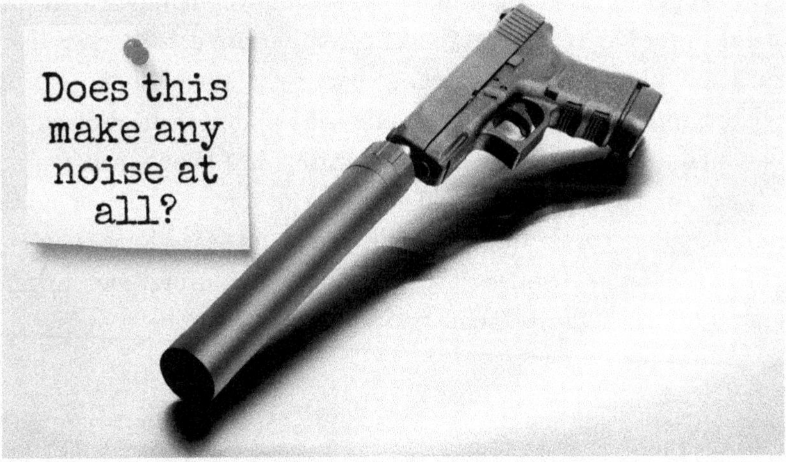

Here's a brain teaser: What's louder, an old-school alarm clock (smartphone alarms don't count for this exercise) or gunshots using silencers? To make this easier, you can count either the normal weekday alarm volume or the special Monday morning version. While we may not understand the underlying science, we all know Monday morning alarms are, in fact, measurably louder.

Got an answer? Gun silencer or alarm clock? If that first one was too easy, how about the comparison between a balloon popping and a firearm suppressor? Let's explore.

But first, a quick note on the terminology. Some folks take great offense at people referring to these devices as "silencers," but technically speaking, that's the correct term. It's right there on the 1909 patent by inventor Hiram Percy Maxim. In more modern times, the term "suppressor" has come into favor as it is more descriptive of what a silencer does.

THE SCIENCE OF SILENCERS

The science behind gun silencers is actually pretty straightforward and can be explained by a party balloon.

Imagine blowing up a balloon and, assuming you have reasonable finger dexterity, tying a knot to keep it sealed. Now, pop it with a pin. What happens? That's right. Bang! You cause the family cat to seek treatment for PTSD. Can cats benefit from service dogs? I guess that's a question for another day, so let's go back to balloons.

Now, imagine filling up that same balloon, but instead of tying a knot, hold the "nozzle" closed with your fingers. At your leisure, gradually let the air out. While you might hear some hissing or noises reminiscent of gross bodily functions, you won't hear a loud bang.

Congratulations, you've just made a silencer using your fingers. Since there's no gun present, the ATF won't even be hunting you down.

PRESSURE NOT FIRE

The "why" behind this may be a little surprising. You might think the noise of gunshots is related to the "explosion" (really just a very rapid conflagration), and it is, but not because of the flames and such. Just like the balloon example, the noise of a gunshot results from the rapid equalization of pressure levels.

An inflated and sealed balloon contains air at a greater pressure than what surrounds it on the outside. When you pop it, the high-pressure air rapidly expands, creating a big noise. In the other scenario, when you release the balloon's air gradually, there is no sudden release of pressure, so there is no significant noise.

GAS AND SILENCERS

When you shoot a gun, a massive amount of high-pressure gas exits the muzzle all at once. Ipso facto E. Pluribus unum, lots of noise.

A silencer does nothing more than help slow down the release of that expanding cloud of gas as it exits the muzzle. Internal baffles in the silencer encourage the gas cloud to swirl around a bit and even cool down, at least a little, before it makes its way out the muzzle end of the silencer tube. Simple, right?

HOW LOUD IS A SILENCER?

Given the volume of gas and the speed of the underlying chemical reaction that causes a bullet to fly, a silencer can't be as effective as slowly releasing the air from a balloon, but it sure does help.

For example, a common handgun creates about 160 dB of noise level at the muzzle. When a suppressor is added, that level is reduced to about 130 dB. That may not sound like much, so it's important to remember decibels are measured on a logarithmic scale so that 30 dB reduction doesn't lower the sound by 18 percent, but rather orders of magnitude. Explaining the scale another way, going from 10 dB to 20 dB doesn't double the noise; it increases it by a factor of 10.

So, silencers quiet gunshots a lot, but how does that compare to other common noises?

NOISE COMPARISONS

Let's consider some actual sound-level examples to set perspective.

A gunshot in a Hollywood movie, detective series or the nightly news is, as we all know, 0 decibels. Miraculous, isn't it?

The dramatic whispering by that same action movie's hero is

about 30 dB. That's a real number. A normal human-to-human conversation measures about 60 dB.

Got a lawn? Your gas mower generates about 107 dB, while a chain saw delivers about 120. Even a car horn (up close) measures 110 dB.

That Megadeath concert you saw in high school would peak around 115 dB.

Even your old-school alarm clock ruins your morning with 80 or more dB.

MYTH... BUSTED

So, what have we learned? A suppressed gunshot is significantly noisier than lots of really loud things like chainsaws, jackhammers and car horns. The next time you watch a movie and don't hear the gunshots, you can call foul with confidence.

Oh, about that balloon pop? One Canadian study measured the peak level of a popping balloon at a whopping 168 dB. There's a lot more to "loudness" than the instantaneous peak level, so you don't have to boycott birthday parties. On the other hand, it's probably not a good idea not to stab balloons right next to your ear.

MOTHS TO MALFUNCTIONS: ORIGIN OF COMPUTER BUGS

In computer lingo, a "bug" is a mistake in the code causing unexpected behavior. You know, like the famous Windows blue screen of death. Somewhere in the millions of lines of nitty-gritty computer instructions are some flaws, which, under a convoluted combination of circumstances, can cause a crash. Other computer bugs can just cause unexpected results, but even those can have major consequences.

BUGGY EXAMPLES

For example, the "biggest" computer bug was Y2K. For those of you not yet born, during the run-up to January 1, 2000, people lost their minds over the potential for catastrophe.

Many, or perhaps most, software coders used a two-digit field to store the year since they didn't foresee their programs being used far into the future, and the practice saved computer memory, which was far less plentiful and orders of magnitude more expensive at the time.

So, for example, "73" was used to indicate the year "1973." Problems arise when the year becomes "2000" as many computers would store just "00," calculating the date as "1900." While the fears of banks crashing, planes falling out of the sky, and nuclear missiles launching themselves never materialized, the scare did cost billions of dollars and the necessity of software rewrites worldwide.

Computers are technically stupid in that they do whatever you tell them, even if the inputs defy logic or represent an obvious (to us) error. While the Hubble Space Telescope debacle was the result of a manufacturing flaw, the Mars Orbiter's cause of death was a computer bug. In 1988, the Mars Climate Orbiter incinerated itself in the thin Martian atmosphere because it calculated the wrong entry angle to achieve orbit. Actually, the onboard computer did precisely what it was told, but somewhere in there, programmers mixed up imperial and metric units of measurement, skewing the positioning calculations by 100km.

One famous bug created history's wealthiest person—even if only for a hot second. In 2007, a programming error in PayPal's software delivered 92 quadrillion dollars to one user. That's 1,000 times more than the GDP of planet Earth. Alas, Pennsylvania resident Chris Reynolds didn't spend it quickly enough, and his account was reset to... zero. Easy come, easy go.

PRE-COMPUTER BUGS?

We think of bugs as idiosyncrasies of computers, but the term was used to represent flaws or glitches long before the first vacuum tube or transistor added any digits. The term "bug," meaning something is awry in the system, actually predates the electric light bulb.

Thomas Edison frequently used the term to describe mechanical and electrical problems while puttering around his Menlo Park lab. In an 1878 letter to Western Union President William Orton, Edison wrote, "I did find a 'bug' in my apparatus, but it was not in the telephone proper." In this case, Edison quoted the word bug as he really did find bugs in the wiring of one of his new telephone designs.

FINDING A COMPUTER BUG!

Computer programming pioneer Rear Admiral Grace Hopper, USN, was working with an early computer at Harvard University all the way back in 1947. The Mark II machine was spitting out consistent errors, so the team investigated the hardware. Like Edison before, someone found an actual bug fouling up the electronic connections. A team member taped the dead moth into the log book with a note saying, "First actual case of a bug being found."

Grace Hopper, her place in history cemented through groundbreaking work on the development of computer languages, wasn't the person who found this bug, but her presence at the incident likely helped make the story of the first known computer "bug" famous.

A bug in the system, indeed.

THE BUTTERFLY EFFECT: DO LITTLE THINGS CAUSE BIG OUTCOMES?

If a butterfly flaps its wings in the forest, scaring the crap out of an elusive Yeti, who takes off and plows into a tree, knocking it over, does it make a sound? I have no idea, but according to the butterfly effect theory, a seemingly inconsequential action, like a butterfly flapping its wings in one place, can lead to shockingly impactful results in a different place.

FLAPPING TORNADOES

While the theory has been around for a couple of hundred years in one form or another, or at least the basics of a small action having a much greater effect elsewhere through some convoluted chain of events, it gained more of its modern definition thanks to a mathematician and meteorologist.

His name was Edward Norton Lorenz, and according to the stories, his original theory had more to do with a bird in one place, ultimately causing a tornado somewhere else far away, thanks to the vagaries of weather patterns and lots of interconnected cause and effect. Either a slick Madison Avenue PR agency or, more likely, a friend suggested he communicate this idea using the butterfly wings analogy to give the story more punch, and here we are.

WHAT'S THE BUTTERFLY EFFECT?

So, how does the Butterfly Effect work? Here's an example.

A low-flying butterfly flaps its wings, ever so slightly shifting a light breeze just enough to move a discarded lottery ticket into a man's line of sight. He picks it up and checks the numbers. A win!

With the winnings from that lottery ticket, young and ambitious entrepreneur Johann Verheem has some extra cash to fund his inventive passions.

Seeing a big market opportunity for an awkward and sexually suggestive exercise fad product, Verheem invents and markets the Shake Weight.

The commercials spread virally, leading to satires on *Saturday Night Live* and *South Park*, among others.

Verheem's new company, FitnessIQ, sells some two million Shake Weights.

Customers realize they've purchased an utterly ridiculous product and begin to donate the barely-used exercise gimmicks to local thrift stores.

Goodwill donation bins are overwhelmed with discarded devices, and they pile up on the shelves by the hundreds.

Your local Goodwill store closes for reconstruction due to an unexpected collapse of shelving units. Dozens of dollars worth of inventory is destroyed.

While this story paints the picture, I'm not entirely sure it's true. But there are plenty of very real-world events that seemingly transpired based on the tiniest shift in circumstances.

PAINTINGS OR WORLD WAR?

One of the most famous examples of the Butterfly Effect involves the world's worst sort of villain—Adolph Hitler.

With dreams of a career as an artist, young Hitler produced hundreds of paintings and sketches in his youth, many during his years living in Vienna from 1908 to 1913. In addition to paintings, Hitler created and sold hand-drawn and colored postcards to eke out a living.

In 1907 and again in 1908, Hitler applied to the Academy of Fine Arts Vienna. Both times, his application was rejected. "Rejected" is a polite way of saying, "Oh, hell no!" One American journalist, John Gunther, wrote about Hitler's paintings, "They are prosaic, utterly devoid of rhythm, color, feeling, or spiritual imagination. They are architect's sketches: painful and precise draftsmanship; nothing more."

Keep in mind this was in 1936 before Hitler became the world's most hated man, so the critique had little basis in simply hating Hitler. After one compassionate professor suggested Hitler might succeed as an architect, the young man flatly refused as that would require more schooling. According to the story, he was ticked and became disillusioned, bordering on bitter.

As the story goes, Hitler became cranky during this era, wandering the streets of Vienna, stewing in anger and voicing his opinions that the Jewish people were to blame for the world's troubles. The rest is history.

But as we all know, art is more than a bit subjective. What if Hitler's academy application had landed on the admissions desk on a happier day, and one or more on the acceptance committee had considered his work with a more open mind? Perhaps the coffee was lousy that morning. Who knows?

World War II resulted in nearly 100 million overall casualties. Would that unfathomable loss of life been avoided had Hitler been accepted to art school? It sure is hard to imagine a similar rise to power from a starting point of painting street scenes in the classroom. Except for that guy who cut off his own ear, painters seem to be pretty mellow folks.

CARATS DEMYSTIFIED: A WEIGHTY EXPLANATION

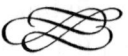

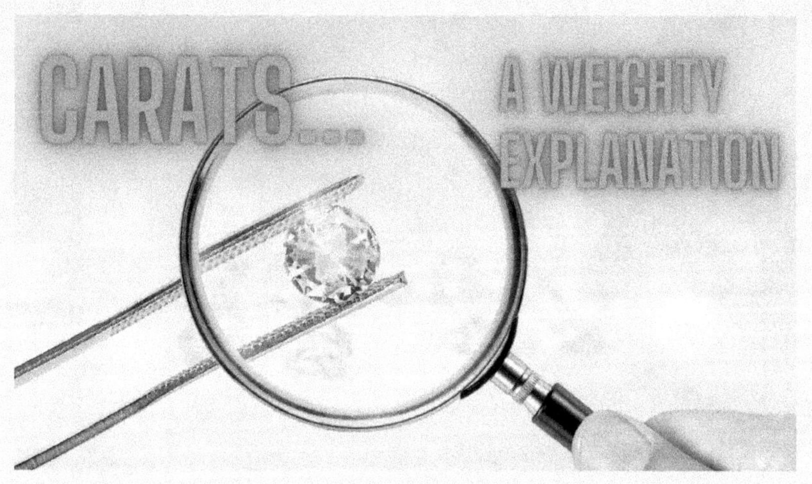

Does your marriage amount to a small hill of beans? If there's a diamond engagement ring in the picture, then technically speaking, yes.

As many generations of suitors well know, a discussion of carats is a sure way to invoke anxiety, fear and possibly bankruptcy. While true love should negate the need to maximize the carat equation, the decision over the number of carats for an engagement diamond brings about as much stress as a *60 Minutes* crew showing up at one's door.

So, what are carats? Why do we weigh diamonds in carats? And what's this about a marriage amounting to a hill of beans? Read on; I promise we'll bring it all together.

CARAT WEIGHT MATH

A carat is just a unit of weight, like a pound or ton. But when using the word "carats," we're generally talking about gemstones, and it's a rare event indeed to measure a blue diamond by the pound. The largest uncut diamond on record (the Cullinan Diamond) tipped the scale at 1.37 pounds, and that was before cutting. After being cut into multiple finished diamonds, the largest was just .117 pounds or 530.2 carats. For the rest of us, much smaller units of measure are in order.

A pound represents 2,267.96 carats, so a carat is not very heavy. To put that in perspective, the largest cut diamond is the Golden Jubilee, which weighs in at 545.67 carats. For reference, the Hope Diamond we gawk at in the Smithsonian weighs just 45.52 carats. That's about one-one-hundredth of a pound or just under a third of an ounce.

If you wanna go metric, a single carat is a fifth of a gram. That's about one-fifth the weight of a paper clip or roughly equivalent to 10 grains of rice before you add water.

If you're in the gemstone-buying mode, there's one more thing you ought to know. A carat is divided into 100 points, so a point is 1/100th of a carat. That covers all those engagement rings between 1 and 2 carats. Yes, jewelers use peculiar measurements.

WHY CARATS?

The whole concept of "carats" is a bit mysterious. Why not just use pounds, ounces, grams or maybe milligrams? I don't know; it's all Greek to me.

And that's part of our answer. The word "carat" does originate from a Greek word—keration—translating to "carob seed."

And here's the kicker. Gemstones certainly aren't new—people have been coveting them for centuries, as evidenced by all the ancient world museum exhibits and the whole idea of buried treasure. For centuries, people have been buying and selling them, so a reliable means of weight measurement was needed.

As it turns out, carob seeds are surprisingly consistent in weight, considering they're part of a bean-like pod growing on... carob trees. Each seed weighs very close to—you guessed it—one carat or .2 grams. Sure, as a product of nature, the seeds can vary a bit, but nothing like, say, an apple or orange. They're pretty consistent in weight, at least enough to serve as a measurement standard before the invention of digital scales.

PONTIFICATIONS

So, now, is your marriage worth a hill of beans? Let's hope so, assuming you made the conversion from carob seeds to diamonds.

If you're worried about presenting a "smallish" ring to a prospective life partner, consider describing it in points instead. "Honey, it's a 20-point diamond!" Yes, that's kind of like increasing the font size to make your English composition page count goal, but hey, desperate times call for desperate measures.

I can't help but notice a one-carat diamond weighs about the same as the medication in a single headache-killing Advil tablet—200 milligrams. Coincidence? I'm pleading the Fifth on that one and withholding comment.

A TIME FOR LONGITUDE: NAVIGATION SOLVED

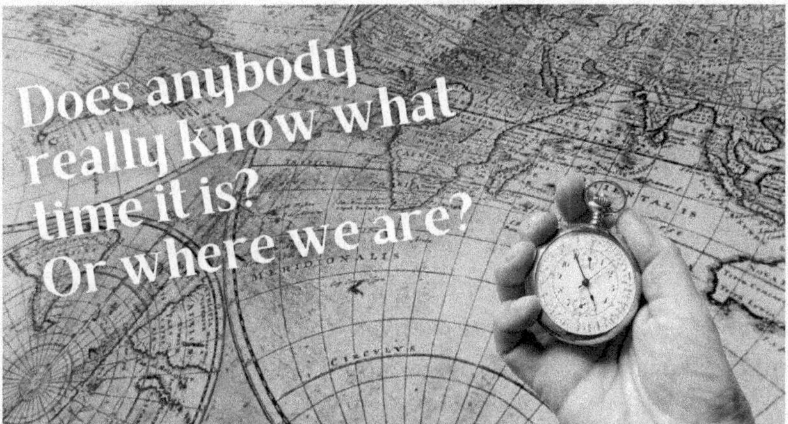

All were lost—always. We listen in awe to stories of the great ocean explorers and navigators from times past, but the fact is, they never really knew where they were.

Those shiny brass nautical instruments that no one really understands only provide some of the information required to figure out where you are. To fix your position on the big blue ball, you need to know both your latitude (how high or low on the ball you are relative to the equator and poles) and longitude (how far around the ball you've traveled from some defined starting point).

As we'll see, the former is easy to figure out and ruled by the laws of nature. The latter is somewhat arbitrary and gave humanity fits for centuries.

THE PROBLEM ILLUSTRATED

Suppose we're driving west on Route 27 to see the World's Largest Ball of Twine in Cawker City, Kansas and have the following directions. "Keep driving west until you see it. You'll know you're halfway there when you see the International Horned Toad Museum on the left."

During the day, this would present no problem. It might take you 10 minutes or hours, depending on how fast you're driving, but the visible landmarks will help you reach your destination, and once you see the halfway landmark, you'll have a vague idea of how far you still have to drive. You can figure out how long you have yet to travel based on your speed and how long it took to reach the halfway mark.

Now imagine doing the same navigation in the pitch dark with no headlights. Oh, and your speedometer is broken. You might see a couple of Taco Bells, but you'd drive right on by the World's Largest Ball of Twine as it and the museum both close at 6 PM and would be dark. You'd have no way of knowing where exactly you are relative to your destination. You might have miles yet to go, or perhaps you already passed it.

Ocean navigation was much like this back in the day.

The problem of finding the world's largest ball of twine in the dark boils down to time and velocity. If you knew it was 30 miles away from your current location, you could use your speed and time elapsed to calculate your position and remaining distance. If careful with the math, you could (in theory) blindly turn left at the precisely calculated time to enter the parking lot, even if it wasn't visible. Ever see that movie, *Hunt for Red October*? Sean Connery did something like that while navigating through underwater canyons in a submarine.

And therein lies the problem faced by, well, everyone sailing the seven seas back in the day. With no reliable speedometer, accurate clocks, or visible landmarks, you really didn't know where you were, much less when you'd arrive.

CHANGES IN LATITUDE, CHANGES IN LONGITUDE

Latitude is easy in comparative terms. Earth is mostly round but a little fatter around the middle, thanks to its rotation. While the equator is still an arbitrary line, there's some substance behind its location. It's equidistant from the north and south poles, and at noon along equator locations, the sun is directly overhead. As you define latitude lines, you create concentric circles decreasing in size as you get closer to the poles, and those lines are parallel—never intersecting. Wherever you are on Earth, the distance to the next latitude line is consistent.

Longitude lines are different. Not only do they run from pole to pole, they're not parallel. At the poles, longitude lines touch. At the equator, they're as far apart from each other as they can get. So, at different latitudes, you'll have different distances to the next longitude line. So, longitude lines represent relative "distance" around the sphere of Earth.

But the big deal for this discussion is longitude demarcations have no natural "starting" position. The beginning of longitude measurements could start in a line passing through Toad Suck, Arkansas or Narvik, Norway. It just doesn't matter. Longitude lines measure how far around our sphere we're located from any arbitrary starting point of longitude definition.

Today, we use a line passing through the Royal Observatory in Greenwich, England. That line, running from pole to pole, right through the observatory break room, is what we call zero degrees longitude. Besides defining location, this line is the anchor for time zone definitions around the world.

DOES ANYBODY REALLY KNOW WHAT TIME IT IS?

Here's where things get interesting. It's fairly easy to determine when it's 12 noon, wherever you are. By definition, the Sun is as high as it can get in the sky. Unless you're on the equator, it won't be directly overhead, but there's always a "highest point" on the arc determined by your current latitude. So, even before the era of quartz watches, it was fairly easy to get an accurate fix on the time of 12 noon by looking up. Even with an inaccurate shipboard clock, early navigators could re-calibrate it every day at noon, so it only had to keep somewhat accurate time for 24 hours.

TIME FOR LONGITUDE POSITION

Now, consider that a day has 24 hours, and this is defined by the rotation of the earth, so a longitude position could be defined by knowing the time at whatever place we defined as zero longitude. If we know it's 12 midnight in Greenwich, England, and it's noon wherever we are, then we must be precisely halfway around the world from the starting point of Greenwich.

Since the earth rotates, time represents distance around the globe. Every hour, we rotate 15 degrees around as defined by 360 degrees for a full rotation divided by 24 hours.

So, one way to accurately figure out your longitude position is to have the ability to keep "home" time precisely on the ship so you know the time from your starting point and the time where you are right now. While land-based clocks have been fairly accurate for centuries, it was much harder to keep accurate time at sea. Pendulum clocks, like the big Grandfather versions, can keep time within a minute per day but don't do so well in the rocking motion of a boat. Salt air, humidity and changing temperatures also wreaked havoc on old mechanical timepieces.

TIME FOR BIG MONEY

In the age of intrepid explorers and folks out to make big bucks in global trade, knowing position while at sea was a very big deal. In fact, it was frequently a matter of life and death. In 1707, a squadron of British ships ran aground, resulting in the deaths of over 1,000 sailors because the ships were closer to land than predicted. The bottom line was that Admiral Cloudesley Shovell and his navigators couldn't determine precisely where they were.

To overcome the navigation problem, governments began offering cash prizes for solutions to the longitude navigation problem. Kings Philip II and III of Spain started in the 1500s, followed by Holland, and by the 1700s, England.

By the 18th century, two methods were in serious contention for the money: the use of lunar distance, relying on celestial observations, lots of data tables, and hours of calculation. The second method was simply figuring out how to keep accurate time. To get a usable longitude fix, seaboard clocks had to be accurate to within several seconds per day—a seemingly unattainable feat at the time.

ENTER JOHN HARRISON

Leave it to a crafty carpenter and clock-maker to persevere in the workshop. No, his name wasn't Joe Timex, but rather John Harrison. Creating a series of five chronometers aptly named H-1 through H-5, it was iteration H-4 that won him the English prize.

Not surprisingly, the powers to be got all tight-fisted when Harrison finally succeeded in solving the longitude problem in a practical way. Because politics. After taking his claim to Parliament, he finally got the cash in 1773.

FINAL ANALYSIS

It pays to wear a watch.

But seriously, until the advent of modern positioning methods like GPS, it was simple timekeeping that enabled accurate global navigation. A fix on the time and some very simple math changed the world as we know it.

The next time you meet a clockmaker, buy them a cookie.

HOW HOT IS LAVA?

We all know lava must be hot, so no mystery there. According to Merriam-Webster, it's "molten rock that issues from a volcano or from a fissure in the surface of a planet." The molten rock part implies something much hotter than they used on that short-lived game show, "The Floor is Lava."

So, how hot is lava? Can you fry eggs on it? How about ribeye steaks? Will it melt beer cans? Is it an effective way for mob enforcers to dispose of dead bodies? Inquiring minds want to know.

LAVA UNEARTHED

Lava is just molten rock, usually loaded with lots of silica-type materials and random assortments of other elements like iron, magnesium, calcium, sodium, and all the other "iums." It's really hot dirt, if you will.

Typical lava, as if lava is ever common, has a viscosity level similar to ketchup. Think of viscosity as the "thickness" of it. Water pours easily and doesn't maintain its shape when it lands on the table. Ketchup sometimes requires whacking the bottle to come out, and when it does, it maintains its lumps when it lands. As we'll see in a minute, you could theoretically keep hot lava in a glass ketchup jar, as glass doesn't melt until it reaches 2,500 to 3,000 degrees Fahrenheit.

LAVA IS SO HOT RIGHT NOW...

If you want to know the numbers, you can assume a range depending on the source and makeup of the lava in question. Temperature as its projectile vomited from the earth might range from 1,400 to 2,200 degrees Fahrenheit. Unless you've touched a hot stove approaching 2,000 degrees recently, the numbers probably don't tell you much, so let's add some context.

HOT STUFF

Kitchen stoves can get near the temperature neighborhood of lava—sort of. Electric stove burners can reach 1,500 degrees, give or take. Natural gas stove flames can approach 2,000 degrees. However, that doesn't mean your pan or food inside comes anywhere close to those temperatures. The burner and pan reach equilibrium long before those temperatures are reached, so we're referring to temperatures that can be generated by the element or flame.

Jet engines are pretty hot. The exhaust from Air Force One's engines varies with ambient temperature conditions, but you might assume an external exhaust temperature of about 1,100 degrees Fahrenheit. If you want to go Maverick and ignite the afterburners on the F-14 Tomcat's engines, that'll significantly increase the immediate exhaust temperature to somewhere in the 2,700-degree range.

On the high side are all those rocket engines used in SpaceX launches. For example, the Falcon Heavy engines contain temperatures in the 6,500 degrees Fahrenheit range, but by the time the hot stuff comes out of the engine nozzle, it's cooled significantly to 2,700 or so.

FIRESIDE LAVA

Perhaps the closest everyday temperature comparison to erupting lava is the typical campfire. To be sure, it needs to be a good one, not some flimsy excuse using fake logs from the local Safeway.

If you build a good bonfire and let it mature for a while, developing a smokin' hot set of embers in the base, you might measure the following temperatures.

The bright orange or reddish flames erupting from the top of our Eagle-Scout-worthy fire should be between 600 and 800 degrees Fahrenheit. While the flickering flame tips look impressive, the hottest stuff is generally at the base.

Moving closer to the source of the flames, the whiter flames right near the wood, especially down in the coal area, can exceed 2,000 degrees Fahrenheit. That's erupting lava territory right there.

There's an easy way to find out if you've got a competitive fire going. Aluminum melts at about 1,200 degrees Fahrenheit, so if your beer can melts in the coals, your fire is hot. Be aware it takes a while for the can to get up to temperature, and you never really know exactly what kind of alloy your beverage can of choice is made from. So, be patient. Several minutes seem to do the trick. Don't ask me how I know.

MOB ENFORCERS

As for lava being a viable snitch disposal mechanism for mob enforcers, the answer isn't quite so clear. Cremation requires temperatures in the 1,600 to 1,800-degree range, but the process takes a couple of hours to complete. So, barring the whole logistics problem of finding an active volcano nearby...

PART VI
HISTORY

Study history, study history—in history lie all the secrets of statecraft.
Winston Churchill

I don't think much of a man who is not wiser today than he was yesterday.
Abraham Lincoln

THE STICKY TRUTH BEHIND TAR AND FEATHERING

Today, we bandy about the term "tar and feathering" to indicate public shaming or humiliation. In the not-so-distant past, tar and feathering was a more physical way to show extreme dissatisfaction. Especially during the revolutionary years, it was a crowd (or more like an angry mob) favorite meant to expose and punish bad behavior, disloyalty, or increasingly unpopular support of crown policies. Think vigilante justice for perceived crimes that don't warrant capital punishment. The end result was not only public embarrassment but a not insignificant amount of pain and suffering.

THE PROCESS

The process is no more complex than the name. The victim is stripped, usually to the waist, but on special occasions, entirely and covered with hot tar. Not the roadside stuff, but pine tar, used at the time as an adhesive and to fill the seams in wooden boats and ships. Once the victim was adequately sticky, they'd be covered in feathers.

Pardon the language, but the bottom line was... this sucked.

If you've ever grabbed a freshly cut log oozing with sap, you know precisely how sticky it is and how hard it is to remove from your skin. Now add semi-permanently attached feathers and the spectacle of morphing into a large bird with second and third-degree skin burns. Not fun. And everyone knew you'd been in hot water for some reason or another. There's no hiding the tar and feathering treatment.

PINE TAR

When we think of tar in these modern times, images of roadside crews cooking that smelly stuff come to mind. Typical road "tar" is heated to 250 to 275 degrees Fahrenheit. Remember, water boils at just 212.

While pine tar is not nearly as hot as the highway stuff, it's still plenty uncomfortable. The melting point of pine tar varies with the type and composition of the substance but ranges from 194 to 300 degrees Fahrenheit. That's hot.

HOW HOT ARE WE TALKING?

To put those temperatures in perspective, a hot tub that's "human safe" and won't scald you maxes out at about 104 degrees Fahrenheit.

While hot tubs can feel uncomfortably hot, one in the factory-recommended temperature range is unlikely to cause burns, so let's consider some other data points.

McDonald's is known for its piping-hot coffee (this is a selling point), and these days, word on the street is the appropriate temperature for their fresh Joe is between 167 and 176 degrees Fahrenheit. It used to be hotter until the famous Liebeck v. McDonald's case, where a woman sued the company for medical damages after receiving third-degree burns when she spilled a cup of hot coffee in her lap. In those days, the suit alleged the company served coffee hotter than other industry players, possibly in the 180 to 190-degree range.

So, whatever the nature of the specific pine tar used in tar and feathering, it's likely it was plenty hot enough to cause painful burns on contact. As for removing it? It's not just uncomfortable; you're going to lose skin.

WHY?

It's hard to argue the punishment factor of tarring and feathering as it's a painful and messy process, but perhaps the real appeal to those who inflicted the practice was the "message" component. In a time when the populace was divided between support of and rebellion against the crown, it was perceived as an effective way to show displeasure to those who violated boycotts against England or engaged in other activities not in support of the revolution.

A CONSTITUTIONAL PARTY

When the argument was over, and copies of the Constitution were being prepared for signing, the boys took George Washington out to celebrate at the nearby City Tavern. Apparently, it was quite a party, and we know this because someone saved the actual bar tab—seriously!

Just some of the items on the bill for "55 Gentlemans" are the following:

- *54 Bottles of Madera*
- *60 of Claret ditto*
- *8 ditto of Old Stock*
- *22 Bottles of Porter ditto*
- *8 of Cyder ditto*
- *12 ditto Beer*
- *7 Large Bowels of Punch*

The bill also includes line items for broken glasses and decanters. Oh, and that list doesn't include the booze for the musicians—that was itemized separately. Sounds like quite a celebration!

A BRIEF HISTORY OF GUNPOWDER

Contrary to popular belief, the history of gunpowder did not originate in 2267 on a small planetoid somewhere in the Milky Way galaxy. In the famous *Star Trek* (the original series) episode "Arena," never-say-die Captain James T. Kirk uses materials scrounged on the planet—charcoal, sulfur and saltpeter (potassium nitrate)—to make his own impromptu gunpowder to defeat a Gorn Captain intent on dismembering the good Star Fleet hero.

As a side note, Kirk used diamond chunks as the most expensive cannon projectile ever and fired the whole shebang from an improvised bamboo cannon. His cannon didn't explode because, apparently, space bamboo has far greater tensile strength than earth bamboo. Be sure to remember that next time you're cruising around the galaxy and leave your Phaser behind in the shuttle.

Anyway, to get back to the story, Kirk knew his history because he recalled the ancient explosive/propellant recipe devised way back in... well, no one knows quite for sure. You see, gunpowder is so old, the history is a bit fuzzy, and that always makes for an interesting story.

ELIXIR OF LIFE... AND DEATH

Sometimes, practical inventions come from ambitious yet unrelated undertakings. The space program brought us artificial limbs, the Dustbuster, LASIK surgery, memory foam, baby formula ingredients, solar power cells, water filtration, invisible braces, and, regrettably, freeze-dried foods.

Details are sketchy, but some accounts refer to a Chinese alchemist mixing three powders, leading to violent combustion as early as 147 AD. Over the next few hundred years, saltpeter experimentation and production continued with efforts to purify other substances and create gold. You know, that old chestnut about making infinite wealth from junk lying around.

Arguably, potassium nitrate is the part of gunpowder that yields the bang, and surprisingly, that ingredient has been in the experimental pot forever. The Nuniya & Labana caste in ancient India (early hundreds AD) used it to create noxious smoke and, according to legend, weaponized the fumes in battle to poison, or at least discourage, the enemy. One thing many saltpeter producers had in common was their attention to poop. Whether by bat guano, animal, or even human doo-doo, saltpeter production often relied on, well, you get the idea.

By the 9th century (give or take, remember, the history is a bit fuzzy), alchemists of the Tang Dynasty were engaged in an ambitious project to concoct an elixir of life. The experiments involved continued tinkering with potassium nitrate, also known as saltpeter. As the substance proved volatile, it may have had the effect of shortening one's expected lifespan rather than leading to the immortality sought.

Additional experimentation brought in other substances like sulfur and charcoal. Voila! The formal production of gunpowder! One early account relates, "Some have heated together the saltpeter, sulfur and carbon of charcoal with honey; smoke and flames result, so that their hands and faces have been burnt, and even the whole house burnt down."

RECREATIONAL USE... AT FIRST

After putting out the house fire, the Chinese put the discovery of this early "gun" powder (remember, none of this was used for guns at the time) to good use in fireworks and magic tricks. The sorcerer who disappears in a flash and cloud of smoke has always been a crowd-pleaser, even in ancient China.

It didn't take long for enterprising warriors to find martial uses for the invention.

The first use of gunpowder involved adding some punch to traditional arrows by attaching a charge to add drama to the arrow's impact. These fire arrows used early formulations of gunpowder with combustion qualities insufficient to launch or fire anything, so think of the early gunpowder as an extra payload of a bow-launched arrow.

During the Song Dynasty, armorers created hollow tube arrows, which functioned more like rockets. This led to the invention of "fire lances," which used black powder to blast flame and debris from a tube. The concept was technically a bit different than a gun barrel, where the projectile occludes the bore and relies on the pressure created by the burning powder to force the projectile from the muzzle. In any case, potentially lethal debris was launched toward the enemy along with its own conflagration.

Also, during this era, enterprising warriors developed all manner of bombs to be thrown or flung via trebuchet at the enemy. Gunpowder, bombpowder... same difference.

GUN AND CANNON POWDER

While many credit the Europeans with the invention of cannons and hand-held firearms, it was more likely the Chinese and Turks. As early as the 10th century, folks in these regions were making crude, eruptive cannon-like devices. There's a blurry line between tubes that blow fiery stuff out the end and a true "gun," so the specific date at which "fiery" powder became "gun" powder is vague. It's pretty clear legitimate cannons came on the scene in Europe in the 13th century.

As guns and cannons rely on the generation of expanding gas pressure to drive projectiles, two things had to happen with the underlying gunpowder technology.

First, the quality of the mixture itself had to improve and become standardized to generate enough combustion power to do more than create a bunch of rapidly burning flames. Consistency and quality of the black powder charcoal, sulfur and saltpeter blend were critical. Once that was achieved, the focus shifted to creating uniform physical properties.

As gunpowder combustion is driven by the surface area of the material, uniformity of the powder granules was a big deal. Too powdery and rapid fulmination blew up both the gun and the operator. Martial chemists soon learned to create larger and more consistent powder granules to control the rate of burn, at least until the advent of smokeless powder, but that's a story for another day.

THE ONLY SIX STAR GENERAL

I think we can all agree George Washington was our manliest of all military generals. During the nation's Bicentennial, Congress voted to put that sentiment into action, posthumously promoting Washington.

The bill, introduced in June 1976, sailed through Congress, passing the House on August 24 of the same year and then the Senate on September 28. President Gerald Ford signed it into law on October 11, 1776.

If you're not inclined to decipher legislative-ese, the bill's intent is simple. No other General, past or present, shall outrank George Washington. That means he's the nation's only six-star General of the Armies of the United States. That's because we've had five 5-star commanders in our history.

1. George C. Marshall (December 16, 1944)
2. Douglas MacArthur (December 18, 1944)
3. Dwight D. Eisenhower (December 20, 1944)
4. Henry H. Arnold (December 21, 1944)
5. Omar N. Bradley (September 22, 1950)

The 5-star rank only applies during wartime (the highest peacetime General officer rank is 4-star). The first four men were awarded their fifth star during World War II. Omar Bradley earned his in 1950 during the Korean War.

As a side note, should we ever face star inflation and create a modern 6-star general, Washington will automatically be "upgraded" to seven stars.

Here's the original text of the law...

> Whereas Lieutenant General George Washington of Virginia commanded our armies throughout and to the successful termination of our Revolutionary War;
>
> Whereas Lieutenant General George Washington presided over the convention that formulated our Constitution;
>
> Whereas Lieutenant General George Washington twice served as President of the United States of America; and
>
> Whereas it is considered fitting and proper that no officer of the United States Army should outrank Lieu-

tenant General George Washington on the Army list: Now, therefore, be it

Resolved by the Senate and House of Representatives of the United States of America in Congress assembled,

That (a) for purposes of subsection (b) of this section only, the grade of General of the Armies of the United States is established, such grade to have rank and

precedence over all other grades of the Army, past or present.

(b) The President is authorized and requested to appoint George Washington posthumously to the grade of General of the Armies of the United States, such appointment to take effect on July 4, 1976.

WHAT WAS THE DEAL WITH WOMEN'S RIGHT TO VOTE?

Election season is upon us. Wait a tic, it's always election season, isn't it? If politicians spent half as much time doing stuff as running for office and subsequent re-election... Well, on second thought, maybe that's not such a great idea as they get us into enough trouble as it is working part-time.

Anyway, one of the strange things about our election history is that it took a lot of effort over a long time for women to be welcomed into the voting process. Women's Right to Vote? Why didn't anyone think of that before?

THE INCOMPLETE 15TH AMENDMENT

One would think this short and sweet Constitutional Amendment, Passed by Congress on February 26, 1869, and ratified on February 3, 1870, would have solved the women's voting issue.

> "The right of citizens of the United States to vote shall not be denied or abridged by the United States or any State on account of race, color, or previous condition of servitude."

While the 14th Amendment attempted to ban direct voting discrimination, practices continued for quite some time. Those not willing to part from the old ways devised all manner of diabolical policies to target minorities, like poll taxes, literacy taxes, and more.

While not a direct ban on voting, these practices prevented large segments of minority communities from participating in elections. Future congressional acts and court decisions whittled away at these injustices over the next century. The 15th Amendment aimed to settle the discrimination issue once and for all. Sort of.

Note that sex isn't included in the list of voting rights. So far, every reference to voting rights has either outright stated or assumed "males" aged 21 or older. Apparently, voting was still considered a *man's thing*. Maybe frustration with the men was a driver of the 21st Amendment a bit further down the road... Don't shoot the messenger, ladies; I'm just relaying the story as it happened...

SUSAN B. ANTHONY

Susan B. Anthony, with a good deal of help from her friends and associates, prompted Senator Aaron Sargent from California to introduce what would later become the 19th Amendment.

Yes, the 19th Amendment established that the right to vote should not be denied because of one's sex. When the 19th Amendment was ratified in 1920, 15 states, mainly those in the western territories, already recognized a woman's right to vote. Ratification took care of the rest in one fell swoop.

HISTORICAL TIDBITS

Before, during, and after the founding years, women's voting rights were essentially non-existent. The underlying rationale for this was the concept of coverture. William Blackstone explained coverture like this:

> "By marriage, the husband and wife are one person in the law: that is, the very being or legal existence of the woman is suspended during the marriage, or at least is incorporated and consolidated into that of the husband: under whose wing, protection, and cover, she performs every thing."

Yes, if you read that and see it as code for "we're guys, and we want to continue to remain in charge, but we're going to do that using a thinly veiled scheme of defining marriage as a grand and glorious union between man and woman that makes them one voting entity. Oh, and by the way, the man makes the rules and, therefore, casts a vote for the team..." you're probably right. Whatever the reason, votes cast by women remained few and far between.

There were exception conditions in some states for various reasons. For example, single women who owned property could sometimes vote. In other cases, widows were allowed to vote, especially if they independently owned property. Some of the underlying logic was that "since the husband was no longer around to guide her, she ought to be able to vote on her own." Remember, ladies, I asked you nicely not to shoot the messenger.

In some cases, the right to vote was arguably accidental.

Ambiguous language in the state Constitution didn't explicitly limit voting to men only, so women voted in New Jersey from 1797 to 1807, when the state legislature finally banned the practice.

As the Virginia Slims cigarette campaign used to say, you've come a long way, baby. Don't shoot the messenger on that one, either!

A CHRISTMAS STORY ... MYTH?

You know what hurts? When you find out your favorite heartwarming fictional stories aren't true. Such is the case, at least in part, with *A Christmas Story*. The iconic 1983 film tells the story, among others, of nine-year-old Ralphie Parker's Christmas wish for an "official Red Ryder, carbine action, 200-shot, range model air rifle, with a compass in the stock and this thing that tells time." One problem. That Daisy Red Ryder didn't exist—and never had.

DAISY FUN FACTS

As iconic as the Daisy name is by now, forever associated with the cowboy-style BB gun coveted by adventurous kids everywhere, the company kinda "spun" into the BB gun business.

In 1882, The Plymouth Iron Windmill Company began making iron windmills for farmers in Plymouth, Michigan. Four years later, the company was foundering and on the verge of shutting down.

However, Michigan watchmaker and inventor Clarence Hamilton had designed and constructed an all-metal air gun. When Plymouth General Manager Lewis Cass Hough test fired the BB gun, he gleefully exclaimed, "Boy, that's a Daisy!" With his support, the windmill company used the BB rifle as a premium to boost windmill sales—a free air rifle with each windmill purchase.

Before long, the company was making more airguns than windmills and, by 1895, had stopped making windmills altogether. And Daisy was born, setting up a future gleeful Christmas for young Ralphie Parker.

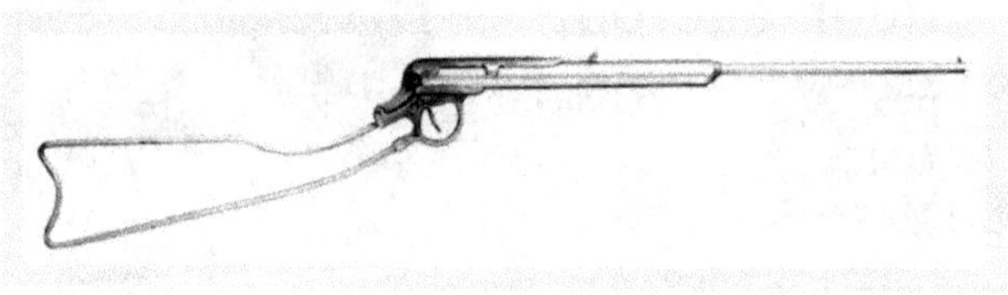

The BB Gun that made a company. Plymouth Windmill's all-metal BB rifle.

RED RYDER OR BUCK JONES?

While no one ever accused Hollywood of getting too worked up about factual reality, the creators of *A Christmas Story* did put the Daisy folks in a bit of a pickle. Writers had concocted the feature set of Ralphie's dream rifle, perhaps based on childhood memories or perhaps out of thin air. In either case, there was no such Red Ryder model with "a compass in the stock and this thing that tells time."

In the past, the company had manufactured a Buck Jones model, which did include a compass. It even had a rudimentary sundial carved into the buttstock. The idea was to insert a match or toothpick into a groove to create the shadow. So, technically speaking, this one most certainly did have "this thing that tells time." Loaded with all these technological wonders, the Buck Jones rifle sold for $2.93 in the 1930s and 40s.

BIRTH OF AN IMAGINARY BB RIFLE

Not a company to pass up an obvious opportunity, Daisy agreed to make a custom run of Red Ryders equipped with the compass and sundial for use in the movie. A whopping six BB rifles were made, one of which was later given to actor Peter Billingsley (Ralphie), while the others landed with various production assistants. Back in 2015 or so, the Christmas Story House & Museum found one of the six and purchased it to round out their movie memorabilia collection.

Since then, Daisy has launched production runs of "Christmas Wish" and "Christmas Dream" Red Ryders. It's not too late; you can buy the 40th (movie) Anniversary edition from the Daisy Museum.

THE DEAD MAN WHO WON WORLD WAR II: OPERATION MINCEMEAT

All's fair in love and war—especially war. The Allies, especially the British, were masters of deception (and sometimes crazy ideas), all in the name of helping to win World War II. From floating tanks to a fake inflatable army, they went to any lengths to fool, deceive, and otherwise confuse enemy forces. Perhaps the most incredible story of all was that of Operation Mincemeat. Translated from military-speak, it's the story of how a dead hobo won World

War II. OK, maybe "won the war" is a bit of an exaggeration, but you have to admit it makes for a great title.

Regardless, the story of Operation Mincemeat might just qualify as one of history's most outrageous misdirections.

DESPERATE TIMES

In 1942, the free world's future still hung in the balance. While Allied forces had managed to slow the Axis juggernaut in North Africa, Europe was still largely under Nazi control. War planners had determined an invasion of Europe through France couldn't happen until sometime in 1944, so the next logical step was to make a bold move into the "soft underbelly" of the continent through the Mediterranean. Logical choices for an initial invasion move included Sicily and Greece.

Just to be on the same page, amphibious invasions against prepared enemy forces are a rotten deal for the invaders. Imagine trying to land on some beach by boat with an entire entrenched army waiting to cut you down. It's a tough gig, to say the least. So, any tactic that might help reduce enemy forces at your chosen landing site could mean the difference between success and failure. What if the Allies could sway German thinking about the site of the forthcoming landing? German military planners might divert defenses to the "wrong" place, improving the odds of invasion success.

00—OPERATION MINCEMEAT

Deception in warfare is the world's second-oldest profession. The always trendy Sun Tzu treatise, *The Art of War,* is chock full of deception strategies. In 1939, the Director of British Naval Intelligence, Admiral John Godfrey, released the "Trout memo," a document outlining a long list of ways to fool the enemy, all based around an analogy of Trout fishing.

While the boss, Godfrey, may have written it himself, it seems more likely that one of his assistants, Ian Fleming, was the author. Yes, that Ian Fleming of James Bond fame. One of the ideas in this memo was to use a fake dead body, presumably a victim of combat or accident, to deliver false information to the enemy. Think of secret plans planted on the body. The enemy discovers the body and plans and thinks it's real because who in their right mind would think of such a deception? Gross.

Fast forward a bit, and we find Royal Navy Intelligence staff officer Ewen Montagu tasked with planning and executing such an operation to divert German resources away from the Allied planned invasion site of Sicily. Montagu and the team settled on the idea of creating a false plane crash or shootdown victim who happened to be an officer carrying plan documents for the forthcoming invasion. Of course, the fake papers would point towards Greece as the intended target—not Sicily.

DEAD BODY, ANYONE?

The operation would require a dead body, preferably one with no strings attached, like family or others who might be curious about the disposition of the remains. Montagu enlisted the help of a London coroner, Bentley Purchase. Now, that's a classic British name, isn't it? I swear I didn't make it up for this story.

Mr. Purchase found a corpse candidate in early 1943. A homeless vagrant, Glyndwr Michael, had died several days after ingesting rat poison. Interestingly, one of the side effects is the development of excess fluid in the lungs—a vaguely supportive bit of evidence that might help convince enemy forces Mr. Michael died from drowning.

THE MAN WHO NEVER WAS... WAS

Obviously, Mr. Michael's real-life story wouldn't do. An itinerant odd-job worker and homeless man would never end up serving as a staff officer, even during the desperation of World War. So, a persona had to be invented.

Montagu and team set about developing the legend of one Captain

William Martin of the Royal Marines. They even gave him an "Acting Major" designation. Little details make a big lie more believable, do they not? The freshly promoted Captain Martin was "assigned" to Combined Operations Headquarters. The idea was to pass off poor Glyndwr as an average staffer, which would help explain the apparent lack of physical fitness expected of a front-line Royal Marine.

The team developed a collection of pocket litter—stuff an actual person might carry around in their wallet to add credibility to their existence. Captain Martin was given a fiancé named Pam, as proven by a wallet photo and a couple of love letters. An MI5 staffer, Jean Leslie, volunteered to model for the shot. Thank you for your service, Ms. Leslie! To add more credible detail, Captain Martin still had a receipt for "Pam's" engagement ring in his wallet. The team added some family letters, an overdraft notice from Captain Martin's bank, and even some London theater ticket stubs—all stuff a wartime man about town might have in his possession.

Montagu went to great lengths to address the details, from personal underwear worn by Glyndwr / Captain Martin to "aging" the documents by rubbing them on his pants for weeks. Deceptions like this weren't new, so the enemy had to be thoroughly convinced.

SECRET SUBMARINE ACTIVITIES

Now, to deliver Captain Martin and his fake documents convincingly to the enemy...

The submarine HMS Seraph was dispatched to the coast of Spain off Huelva, with the body preserved via a special container equipped with dry ice. The Captain and officers read Psalm 39 and slid Glyndwr into the sea, aiding his eventual beach landing by directing the sub's propellers toward the shore.

A local fisherman found "Captain Martin," and the process began. He was autopsied and buried with military honors. The briefcase, with various letters, some referencing false Sardinian operations, eventually made its way to Madrid. Although German sympathizers and agents attempted to gain access to the documents, the Spanish resisted until senior Abwehr agents pressured the Spanish for a discreet look. A week or so after discovery, the Germans managed to get a secret look at the contents and bought the story hook, line and sinker.

Note how the British didn't make it easy for Germany to get their hands on the planted documents. While a risky strategy as it was far from guaranteed the documents would ever make their way to German agents, making it difficult for the Germans added credibility to the ruse.

DID IT WORK?

By all accounts, yes. Adolf Hitler himself referenced the documents while encouraging the movement of thousands of fighter aircraft and numerous divisions of combat troops to Sardinia and the Peloponnesus.

While it's impossible to know the exact impact of Operation Mincemeat, the ultimate invasion of Sicily was successful and accomplished with fewer losses than planners anticipated.

Apparently, dead men do tell tales.

THE REAL STORY OF THE IWO JIMA FLAG RAISING

Sometimes, a moment ascends to the level of iconic historical events. Such is the case with the Iwo Jima flag raising during World War II. Who doesn't recognize the classic triangular lines of men planting an improvised flagpole in the battle-scarred landscape of Iwo Jima? That "simple" flag-raising, the first foreign flag ever planted on Japanese soil, changed the perception of the war in the

Pacific and was associated with the spread of misinformation on a global scale.

While hard to imagine in today's world of instantaneous video news accounts, the US Marine landing on Iwo Jima was one of the first world events where "up to the day" news made its way around the world. In previous World War II battles, citizens back home would hear and see accounts and photos days or even weeks after the fact.

The process was streamlined during the attack on the world's most heavily defended island, and Americans back home hung on every new update, often getting news morning and evening of events that happened within the past 24 hours. While many today remember precisely where they were during the Challenger disaster or the events of 9/11, older generations remember the moment they first saw "the photo."

INVASION

On February 19, 1945, 30,000 United States Marines (to be followed by an additional 40,000 over the coming days and weeks) landed on the black volcanic ash beaches of Iwo Jima. By this time, Japanese defenders had turned the entire island, including Mount Suribachi, into a maze of underground tunnels and caves full of soldiers, mines and booby traps designed to inflict maximum casualties for the Americans.

By the fourth day, constant American bombardment had seemingly quieted down activity on Mount Suribachi, which overlooked the entire landing zone, so after successful reconnaissance by a four-man patrol, Lieutenant Colonel Chandler Johnson called for a 40-man unit, led by First Lieutenant Harold Schrier, to scale Mount Suribachi and, *if they made it,* plant a flag up there.

For reasons unknown, though the mountain still shielded hundreds of Japanese soldiers who could have destroyed the patrol to a man, resistance was nearly non-existent, and the group made it to the top of 554-foot-tall Suribachi.

THE REAL IWO JIMA FLAG RAISING

A small group led by Lieutenant Schrier scavenged a length of water pipe, fastened the American flag provided by Colonel Johnson, and, as what one might expect as part of an official photo shoot, raised it while Marine photographer Lou Lowery took pictures. The process resulted in a series of posed photos of various combinations of the team's leaders and various marines.

Soldiers throughout the landing areas and sailors on offshore ships had seen the patrol inching up the mountain, expecting them to be annihilated, so when the group made the top and raised a flag, cheers erupted from thousands of witnesses.

One problem. These photos and the underlying events had nothing to do with the iconic flag-raising image we all know.

ONCE MORE, FOR THE CAMERAS...

Meanwhile, as they always do, the "brass" was itching to steal the glory. Secretary of the Navy James Forrestal, having just landed on the island, decided he wanted the original flag as a souvenir. Colonel Johnson was, let's say, slightly resistant to that idea, figuring the flag belonged to the battalion. He ordered runner Rene Gagnon to deliver a new flag to the team on top of Suribachi and recover the original before Forrestal snagged it.

Meanwhile, another photographer, Joe Rosenthal, heard about the team's mission to Suribachi's summit and wanted to take his own photos. Heading up the hill with two Marine photographers, he actually encountered Lou Lowery, who was on the way down. Lowery informed him that he had already captured the flag-raising moment, but perhaps Rosenthal might want some good photos of the island from the higher vantage point.

When Gagnon reached the summit with the larger flag, the team began organizing a replacement, substituting the new and larger one for the original to be sent back to Colonel Johnson. The idea was to lower the original flag simultaneously with raising the new replacement—a logistical non-event as the first flag had already been raised.

In an entirely impromptu action, with Marine Harlan Block anchoring the base of the new pole, a group raised the replacement flag while Rosenthal quickly snapped a photo, barely seeing what was in the viewfinder.

The iconic Iwo Jima flag-raising photo we all know was actually the second "replacement" flag-raising. Image: U.S. Marine Corps/National Archives

A "NON-EVENT" SEEN AROUND THE WORLD

As it turns out, Rosenthal had no idea what the impact of his photograph would be. After sending his film to the lab, technicians discovered that light streaks ruined the two pictures adjacent to Rosenthal's big shot. But the classic Iwo Jima flag-raising photo came out perfectly, and editors didn't take long to realize the image's history-changing power.

Almost immediately, the photo made its way around the world, showing up literally everywhere. Seeing that picture, people naturally assumed it reflected the fight in progress and the end of the costly battle for Iwo Jima. Nothing was further from the truth. While a couple of Japanese soldiers popped up on the mountaintop throughout the process, the second flag-raising captured on film was largely an administrative affair—a "non-event." At that moment, at least, the bullets and shells were not flying and the team was not charging enemy positions on the mountain.

Nor did this flag planting signify the capture of Iwo Jima. In fact, the opposite was true. While casualties in those first four days had been astronomical, they represented just the beginning of the ultimate cost of gaining control of the island. By the end, approximately 27,000 Americans and some 18,000 Japanese would be killed, wounded, or declared missing.

That didn't stop the media from fabricating narratives about the flag raising, describing grenades and bullets flying while the brave team assaulted the mountain and planted the flag. The truth never got in the way of a good story. To be clear, the battle as a whole was perhaps one of the most brutal and nastiest on record, just not at the moment and location where that iconic photo was snapped.

A MOM ALWAYS KNOWS

The name of the man at the base of the flagpole, driving it in between the rocks, was no mystery at all to Belle Block. Even though the photo shows only the back side of the Marine, without even a side view of his face, Harlon Block's mother, Belle, recognized him in an instant.

Immediately on seeing the famous newspaper photo, Belle exclaimed to her other son, Ed Jr., "Lookit there, Junior! There's your brother Harlon!" Quite a call, considering the newspapers had no identifications at the time, and Harlon's family had no way of knowing if he was anywhere near Iwo Jima. But Belle was sure, "Oh, that's definitely Harlon. I know my boy."

WHO RAISED THE FLAG(S)?

They say history is alive, and in this case, that narrative plays out. It took until 2018 to (once and for all?) settle the debate over who the Marines are in the photo.

While there were some early mistakes, the long-standing roster of the six flag-raisers pictured in the photo included Rene Gagnon, Harlan Block, Franklin Sousley, John Bradley, Ira Hayes and Michael Strank.

Enter the fog of war.

Over the years, investigation into the identities of the six men in the photo continued. By 2018, the prevailing wisdom was that the group included Cpl. Harlon Block, Pfc. Harold Keller, Pfc. Ira Hayes, Pfc. Harold Schultz, Pfc. Franklin Sousley and Sgt. Michael Strank.

All of the men listed were on the mountaintop that day for the first and second flag raisings, so we're not going to split hairs over who helped stick which flag in the ground.

While some identification details are now in dispute, the outstanding book *Flags of Our Fathers* is a fantastic read. Highly recommended.

PART VII
POLITICS

Just because you do not take an interest in politics doesn't mean politics won't take an interest in you.

Either Pericles circa 430 B.C. or urban legend—we're not exactly sure. The only politician present when these words might have been uttered is Senator Mitch McConnell, and he's not saying.

I looked up the word politics in the dictionary, and it's actually a combination of two words: poli, which means "many," and tics, which means "bloodsuckers."

Jay Leno

PUTTING BIG GOVERNMENT SPENDING IN PERSPECTIVE

Apparently, the plural of 'census' is not 'censii' but if it were, I'd say we've been doing censii forever, or at least since 1790. When the country was founded, a proper census was required to establish the makeup of the House of Representatives. When the results were tabulated, there were about 3.93 million freshly minted Americans.

A spanking new federal government was in place, although much smaller in scope than we're accustomed to. With objectives limited to a handful of things like fighting any necessary wars, setting up a postal system, standardizing weights and measures and protecting natural rights, the budget was modest to say the least. Limited scope or not, these things still cost money, so the government had a budget of about $3.69 million in 1792 dollars. So, the concept of government spending has been a thorn in our side for a while.

COLONIAL EFFICIENCY

If we consider that first national budget in today's dollars, that $3.69 million would translate to about $121 million. You know, inflation.

Doing some quick math, the new federal bureaucracy spent about $30.73 per citizen on various projects. Yes, you read that right. The government spent the equivalent of dinner for four at McRonalds. In today's dollars. And that was **for the entire year**.

PORK-SPLOSION

Things have changed a bit since then. For fiscal year 2024, federal spending hit $6.75 Trillion. That's with a "T," just to be clear. You know, a thousand billion. Of course, we've grown a bit, too, so some of that spending is to cover the additional 342 million folks around here.

However, when you look at the per-person budget, it's apparent our politicians have become just a bit more extravagant. We're long past the dinner with Ronald, as each citizen's share of the budget is now **a whopping $19,508.67 per year.**

PERSPECTIVE

No question about it: our population has grown significantly over the past 234 years—by a factor of 88 if you do the math.

But spending laid a hand on population growth's shoulder and whispered, "Hold my beer." Federal spending has outpaced population growth by just a bit, growing **by a factor of 635** when you consider everything in today's dollars and on a per capita basis.

You could look at the spending explosion in a slightly different way. While the population has grown by a factor of 88, total spending, again in current dollars, has increased by a factor of 55,785.12.

WHAT YOU NEED TO KNOW ABOUT IMPEACHMENT

Impeachment is all the rage these days, although, throughout American political history, only three presidents have earned the coveted impeachment jacket: Andrew Johnson, Bill Clinton and Donald Trump. Richard Nixon may come to mind, but he fell into the "always a bridesmaid, never a bride" category as he resigned from office before the completion of impeachment proceedings.

HISTORY OF IMPEACHMENTS

Here's the kicker. Historically, impeachments have had about as much impact as the Psychic Hotline. To date, no president has ever been removed from office by the impeachment process, although the procedure has given us an infinite supply of off-color jokes. For those who don't have Air Force One Fast Pass tickets, impeachment is much more common. Sixty-some people in lower positions have been impeached, but only 19 of them have endured the entire process. Of those, only eight were ultimately kicked out of office. If you're curious, they were all federal judges.

We're not in the business of arguing for or against impeachment proceedings, so we'll leave that to the legions of cable news show pundits and their seemingly endless and mind-numbing panel discussions.

As I write this, impeachment grenades are crossing each other mid-air over the proverbial aisle. Here, we're going to talk about what impeachment is and how it works. Then, you can make your own judgments about who should and shouldn't be impeached.

THE IMPEACHMENT PROCESS

While we can all agree that Congress generally operates like a preschool where the lunch lady spiked the Turkey Tetrazzini with PCP, in the case of impeachment, it's Congress members who get to be the parents. Simply put, Congress has the ability to put the President (or other "civil officers of the United States") in a political timeout. Actually, it's more like a weaponized time out because not only can Congress issue stern warnings, but they can remove a President from office, take away the plane, and start eviction proceedings from 1600 Pennsylvania Avenue. Hold this thought for a hot second; there's a lot more than a simple impeachment vote required to implement such extreme actions.

So, what is impeachment? If you watch crime dramas like *Law and Order* or follow any politician's career for more than 12 months, you might be familiar with the concept of indictments. An indictment is an accusation. You might think of it as a leveling of charges, kind of like a frustrated parent counting to three before the serious discipline begins.

Here, the parent is the House of Representatives. I know that's tough to swallow, so just stay with me. While the House can, through a vote, impeach a sitting President, the process is not a trial; the completion of it does not represent a conviction, and impeachment isn't even evidence of guilt. After the House finishes impeaching, the process moves to the Senate for a "trial" phase.

CONSTITUTIONAL JUSTIFICATIONS FOR IMPEACHMENT

So, what manner of bad behavior can bring about impeachment? That's addressed in Article II, Section 4 of the United States Constitution. If the thought of reading the Constitution makes you want to fake your own death, get a copy of my book, The Practical Guide to the United States Constitution. Even a career politician can understand it. It's also fun. Now, let's go back to the issue at hand.

> The President, Vice President and all civil Officers of the United States, shall be removed from Office on Impeachment for, and Conviction of, Treason, Bribery, or other high Crimes and Misdemeanors.

You have to give the Founders an A+ for brevity. Those 31 words cover a lot of ground, don't they? The Constitution doesn't go into any more detail over what specifically makes up "high crimes and misdemeanors," but it's been generally understood that impeachable offenses do not have to be a violation of criminal law. When leading the House minority, Gerald R. Ford (you know him, he later became the stumbling president) suggested, "An impeachable offense is whatever a majority of the House of Representatives considers it to be at a given moment in history." For example, some future Oval Office occupant may give the Presidential Medal of Freedom to the cast of *The Real.* While not technically illegal, I think we can all agree the action would cause irreparable harm to the country, so that might be an impeachable offense.

Per Article One of the Constitution, the House of Representatives is solely empowered to begin impeachment proceedings at the federal level. The process is simple, although cable pundits make it seem complicated. After some investigation, which may start just about anywhere, someone in the House of Representatives draws up articles of impeachment. This is nothing more than an itemized listing of bad behavior accusations. Once the articles are filed, the House votes, and if a simple majority of voting members present agree, then the alleged offender has been duly impeached.

CONSEQUENCES, OR NOT, OF IMPEACHMENT

What does that mean? Besides a few headlines and possible political clout impacts, not much. The impeachee still wakes up the next morning and goes to work, just like the day before. The only exception to their normal routine might be a ruthless slashing of their holiday card list.

It's kind of like a United States version of a bollocking. Having been bollocked myself one morning in Scotland, just minutes after a brutal red-eye flight, I now know bollocking involves a lot of noise and threatening words, but with no lasting consequences except to one's pride.

It's the Senate that judges all legal proceedings that follow impeachment. Besides looking stern and speaking to news media about how unpatriotic the offending party is, they get to hear evidence, berate lawyers, and ultimately decide on guilt or innocence.

Two-thirds of the present Senate must agree before someone is deemed guilty. If it happens to be the President of the United States who is getting impeached, then the Chief Justice of the Supreme Court presides over the trial.

While the senators can have a trial to determine whether the impeachment has teeth, their punishment options are limited. Should you ever get impeached, the Senate can only remove and disqualify you from "any office of honor, trust, or profit under the United States."

However, don't think you're off the hook from spending time in the slammer. If you did something illegal, you can still be arrested, indicted, tried, judged, and punished accordingly; it's just not part of impeachment proceedings.

Oh, one more thing. Those handy presidential pardons don't apply to those impeached. Presidents can't pardon themselves or any other impeachees.

THE GREATEST CONSTITUTIONAL AMENDMENT EVER?

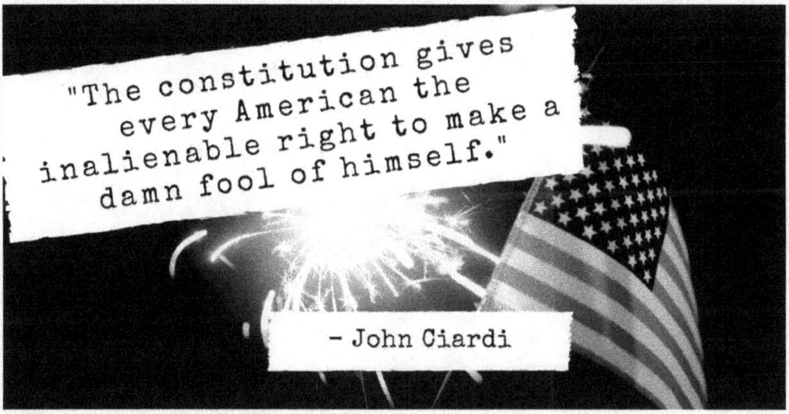

I thought it might be fun to share one of the more amusing stories of a proposed constitutional amendment. On reflection, it does seem to make a lot of sense today…

In 1922, Wisconsin representative Victor Berger proposed a constitutional amendment to abolish the United States Senate. You can sense his frustration level from the preamble to his proposed amendment.

> Whereas the Senate, in particular, has become an obstructive and useless body, a menace to the liberties of the people, and an obstacle to social growth; a body, many of the Members of which are representatives neither of a State nor of its people, but solely of certain predatory combinations, and a body which, by reason of the corruption often attending the election of its Members, has furnished the gravest public scandals in the history of the nation...

Hmm. I might support this one. Perhaps we can resurrect it?

HOW DO POLITICIANS GET RICH? FORTUITOUS LAND INVESTMENTS

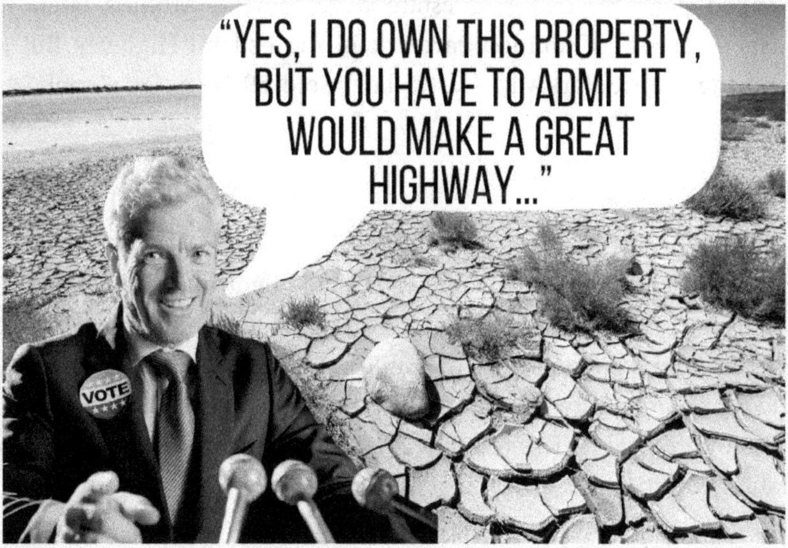

Politicians are among the world's most skilled investors. It's the only possible explanation for the off-the-charts wealth-building success that occurs in the District of DeeSee.

OK, you and I both know that's a load of bull hockey, and there's more at play, so let's explore just exactly how those "public servant" salaries so frequently translate into untold millions. Spoiler Alert: It's not from frugal living and careful investment of coupon savings.

One more thing... Documenting the antics of the political elite could fill the Library of Congress, so we'll address their investment habits in multiple stories likely to also fill any sequels to this book.

Let's start with some examples of fortuitous land investments. With no set price and no disclosure requirements for land deals, it's relatively easy to work the system to benefit the value of one's land holdings while avoiding testimony in front of the Ethics Committee. Then again, they've probably figured out how to monetize that, too.

IF YOU BUILD A PARKWAY, MONEY WILL COME

In 2005, Speaker Dennis Hastert purchased 264 acres near a planned parkway and real estate development. Months later, he pushed for a $207 million earmark in the Federal Highway Bill to fund the Prairie Parkway. Haster later sold 69 acres for a cool $4.9 million.

CAN YOU SPRUCE UP MY OFFICE?

House leader Nancy Pelosi and her husband own an office building in her district in San Francisco. Over the years, different pork projects have had quite an impact on the building, which is valued between $1 and $5 million. Between 2004 and 2011, Pelosi pushed for nearly $1 billion in federal dollars to build a light rail system, with one planned station within prime distance of her property.

In 2006, another $20 million waterfront earmark benefitted the same property.

LET'S KEEP IT IN THE FAMILY

Former Chairman of the Senate Budget Committee, Senator Judd Gregg, directed $66 million to convert Pease Airforce Base into an office park. Oh, the office park was developed by Gregg's brother. Oh, and Gregg also invested in the project, turning a tidy profit.

A BRIDGE TO PROPERTY APPRECIATION

The late Senator Harry Reid purchased a controlling interest in a 160-acre parcel of land owned by a lifelong friend's lubricants business pension fund. He paid the princely sum of $10,000 or $166 per acre for land appraised by the tax assessor at ten times that value. Two years later, a similar adjacent parcel sold for $4,260 per acre—almost 26 times the purchase price of Reid's property.

About six months later, the Senator introduced very specific legislation mightily favorable to the friend's business interests—a proposed law to assist lubricant companies in their dealings with Big Oil. The bill didn't go anywhere and was reintroduced several more times. Nothing ever happened, at least directly. But, Big Oil did get a loud and clear message that Congress was watching their dealings with the smaller lube companies.

Not surprisingly, this very same land turned out to be a gift that kept on giving. As if the purchase at a fraction of the appraised value was not enough, as it turned out, a "purely coincidental" earmark pet project drove some serious appreciation in the property's value.

In 2006, Senator Reid pushed for an $18 million bridge across the Colorado River between Laughlin, Nevada and Bullhead City, Arizona. Neither state had any apparent desire for the bridge, but at least the project drove up prices for Reid's 160 acres. Previously valued somewhere between $250,000 and $500,000 on 2006 disclosure forms, the property was later tagged at somewhere between $1 and $5 million by 2010.

EXPERT HOME SELLER

Rep. Randall Cunningham of California was a member of the House Defense Appropriations Subcommittee. Interestingly, he ended up selling his house to a defense subcontractor for twice its market value.

That's some outstanding salesmanship, isn't it? Better yet, the company provided living arrangements for Cunningham on a luxury yacht free of charge.

You probably won't be surprised to learn that in 2005, Cunningham pled guilty to $2.4 million in accepted bribes, leading to an eight-year prison sentence.

These are just a paltry few examples of how your representatives just might game the system to line their humble servant's pockets.

Stay tuned for a look at some of the other wealth-building strategies. It's all at our expense, so we might as well know what's going on!

ABOUT PRESIDENTIAL CABINET RECESS APPOINTMENTS

I can't help but laugh when I hear about Congress going on recess. Yes, they learned everything they needed to know about life in kindergarten. And yes, they act like they're still there. So, the mental picture of congressional recess usually involves a playground, kick-ball, bullies and maybe some skinned knees.

More recently, congressional recess has ignited a new raging debate. Can a President choose people to fill cabinet positions while the Senate is in recess? How does that work when a whole bunch of people support a president and a different whole bunch of other people oppose the same president, so Senate agreement is nothing but a wish upon a rotunda?

SENATORIAL FUNCTIONS

The Constitution is very clear about certain things. One such concept is the enumeration of governmental powers in general.

As far as a president's appointments (like cabinet members), it is Article II, Section 2 of the Constitution that states, "and by and with the Advice and Consent of the Senate, shall appoint Ambassadors, other public Ministers and Consuls, Judges of the Supreme Court, and all other Officers of the United States."

So, it's pretty clear the Senate has to approve of a President's cabinet picks, and tradition calls for a simple majority vote to do so.

CABINET APPOINTMENTS IF THE SENATE IS CLOSED

The Constitution addresses recess periods too, and the language, also in Article II, Section 2, is equally clear.

"The President shall have Power to fill up all Vacancies that may happen during the Recess of the Senate, by granting Commissions which shall expire at the End of their next Session."

The bottom line is if the Senate isn't happy about a President's cabinet picks, they have two choices. Vote no to the "advice and consent" part or go on recess to delay the debate and subsequent vote. However, the running-out-to-recess strategy only kicks the can down the road—the President can still get his or her cabinet picks, although temporarily.

IF THINGS GET REALLY UGLY

There is a potential nuclear option of questionable constitutionality that may conceivably be used in a cabinet approval battle. Article II, Section 3 contains the following general presidential power.

"...he may, on extraordinary Occasions, convene both Houses, or either of them, and in Case of Disagreement between them, with Respect to the Time of Adjournment, he may adjourn them to such Time as he shall think proper..."

While not specific to cabinet "advise and consent" discussions, and considering this clause seems to refer to disagreement between both houses (the Senate and the House of Representatives), perhaps some legal wrangling might bring Section 3 into play. It's not hard to imagine how such a move might prove counterproductive.

Putting 535 prideful blowhards in a forced timeout likely wouldn't end well for anyone.

IS THE UNITED STATES A DEMOCRACY?

Just because you do not take an interest in politics doesn't mean politics won't take an interest in you.

Either Pericles circa 430 B.C. or urban legend—we're not exactly sure. The only politicians present when these words might have been uttered are Representative Pelosi and Senator McConnell, and they're not saying.

You know how professional arguers on Twitter, sorry, I mean "X," say pithy, annoying, and decidedly final things like, "This is a democracy!" While the good 'ol US of A operates under democratic, and sometimes idiocratic, principles, we're technically a...

CONSTITUTIONAL REPUBLIC

Yeah, I know, more often than not, we seem to operate more like a constipational republic. Think about it. Things never move through the system smoothly; there's a great deal of pain, and nothing short of a high-pressure enema will clear things up.

As the old saying goes, a democracy is two wolves and a sheep deciding what to have for dinner. If you have never read *The Call of the Wild*, the wolves will almost always decide on lamb chops for dinner unless they have coupons for pizza night. And then, the lamb is an appetizer.

In other words, everyone has an equal say and the majority opinion rules. Got 100 citizens? Then, 51 who agree on something call all the shots. Fair, right? This sounds pretty good on paper until you realize that whoever is in the minority has no say at all.

A good example of a modern-day democracy is...

AMERICAN IDOL

Rather than relying on professional talent judges to determine if someone can sing, we rely on pre-teen girls and bots to determine who gets a multi-million dollar recording contract. And herein lies the problem. Pre-teen boys are far more interested in things like playing Call of Duty and trying to date pre-teen girls than texting votes to the American Idol computers, so the pre-teen girls have all the say about who is the next pop idol and who is headed for a career as a chorus singer. The minority group of pre-teen boys who do vote are simply outnumbered and, therefore, have no say in the outcome. It's pre-teen girl mob rule, pure and simple, not to mention a travesty of justice. Someone should appoint a special prosecutor.

IT'S ALL GREEK TO ME

Mob rule without minority representation is just one problem with pure democracy. Just ask the ancient Greeks.

Inspired by Cleisthenes in 507 B.C., the Greeks tried out the whole idea of demokratia (rule by the people). A noble plan for sure, and it certainly inspired variations on the pure democracy idea throughout history. While every person in Athenian society could not vote, all male citizens over the age of 18 could—about 10,000 people.

The primary decision-making body was the Ekklesia (Assembly), which was a rough equivalent to our Congress today. The Ekklesia met in person a whopping 40 times per year, and all 10,000 voting citizens were invited to participate.

Stop and recall the last school board, town council or neighborhood association meeting you attended. Now, imagine someone brought in a small college stadium full of people to bring forth their opinions after having spiked the refreshments with PCP, and you have a picture of a typical meeting.

There was also a Council of 500 (the Boule), selected by random lottery, which met daily and decided what business to bring before the Ekklesia, so the 5,000 or so had at least some guidance and prioritization going into their near-weekly meetings.

As the saying goes, there's nothing new under the Sun, and cracks began to appear in the foundations of the everyone-decides-everything model. The public decision-making bodies began to be swayed into irrational and nation-harming decisions. Slick speeches and, in some cases, bribery, either direct or indirect, by voting to drain national resources in favor of policies that "sounded good" led to a series of consequences for the Athenian empire. After some disastrous mishaps with the Greek Navy, the Macedonians eventually took control. As it turns out, the population as a whole does not do an admirable job of managing the day-to-day business of running wars.

LOUSY LOGISTICS

As the Greeks discovered the hard way, the other problem with a "true" democracy is that everyone has to constantly vote on things.

Even with political technology advances like Twitter, YouTube and TikTok, getting everyone to comment on every decision presents a logistical nightmare. While a pure democratic decision-making process seems to work passably for American Idol, you have to look at the dark side. For example, we elected Clay Aiken as the hottest new pop-performing talent in the country. No one said a democracy isn't without risk.

We're used to pure democracy in action for American Idol, but just imagine for a second this process in action on the political front where we have to decide on issues of national importance.

- Should we invade Liechtenstein?
- Should the new post office in Toad Suck, Arkansas, be named after former Congressman Anthony Weiner, the purported inventor of the Shake Weight?
- Is the group of congresspeople investigating the other group of congresspeople righteous, or are they just acting like a bunch of weenies?

I don't know about you, but I fear the Internet. The internet still hasn't decided who killed JFK or whether or not we actually landed on the moon, although in fairness, it has apparently decided the Kardashians should be awarded somewhere over a billion dollars.

A SOLUTION: THE CONSTITUTIONAL REPUBLIC

One way to solve some of the inherent problems associated with mob rule is to establish a system where the public selects members from amongst themselves to represent them. In theory, these people will allocate more time to understanding the issues, formulating rational policy decisions, and doing all that while getting filthy rich in the process. Also, in theory, this representative form of government protects the rights of the minority.

The underlying idea is that the people remain in control (republican form of government) as they have the power to remove their chosen representatives from office with their votes (democratic process) should they feel so inclined. As for the constitutional part, that's the rule book that defines precisely how the representative system will function and how the rights of the majority and minority will be balanced.

Will it last longer than the Ancient Greek system? Time will tell.

WHY WE DON'T HAVE 11,141 REPRESENTATIVES IN CONGRESS

Fewer of us than ever before are watching the news, but even still, you may have noticed we don't have 11,141 representatives in Congress, all fighting for microphone time while investigating each other.

I suppose we need to unpack that observation just a bit.

THE FOUNDER PLAN

The original plan envisioned by our Founders was for each state to have at least one representative, but not more than one for every 30,000 people.

Back in 1789, there were only 65 members, but the House rapidly filled as the country's population grew. By the turn of the 20th Century, things were getting out of control, and some rural areas were nervous about losing influence to more dense population centers.

If you're math-inclined, you might notice that we have many more people these days than our number of representatives would indicate.

LET'S SEE, CARRY THE ONE...

At the time of this writing, there are about 334,233,854 people in the United States—and that doesn't include the 173 Hollywood actors who have threatened to leave the country if their candidate doesn't win the next election.

If there were one representative in Congress for each group of 30,000 Americans, we ought to have 11,141 Congressional Representatives wandering the Capitol halls and having expensive lunches on our tab.

Obviously, this is not at all feasible. To make things work, we'd have to start importing interns and press secretaries from China. We'd also have to house the House of Representatives at FedEx Field in Landover because the 58,000 seating capacity might just hold our 11,000 self-important buffoons, their pages, staff and cosmetologists. That's a lot of people mobbing the NBC remote broadcast setup every day.

Talk about a Constitutional Crisis. Fortunately...

PROBLEM SOLVED (PARTIALLY)

Fortunately for the Washington news desks of major television networks, some forward-thinking folks invented the Apportionment Act of 1911. This law permanently limited the number of representatives to 435, arguably about 432 too many, but certainly an improvement. Now, as states grow and population shifts, the number of Representatives for each state is determined proportionately by the census, subject to that 435 overall limit.

We've limited their numerical infestation; now, if we could only make them behave...

HOW DO POLITICIANS GET SO RICH? 2: STOCK MARKET MASTERY!

As we reviewed in "Fortuitous Land Investments," politicians are quite skilled at investing their income from (relatively) modest public servant salaries. So skilled, in fact, that many of them become multi-millionaires while in office. We can only hope to learn from their careful investing in the stock market and frugal spending habits...

Insider trading is a pretty straightforward scheme. Someone tells someone else about future news (good or bad) and that someone else makes a profitable stock trade before the general public knows anything about it. Easy money. Also illegal.

Our faithful public servants arguably have plenty of access to insider information, but they also have far more insidious opportunities to make serious bank on the market.

Public companies register to lobby in Washington to win legislative victories favorable to their business. What company leadership wouldn't want to do that? The problem occurs when the very same people who decide what legislation is going to pass or not pass are also able to buy shares in the companies about to be impacted by their actions.

Sound rotten to the core? It is. And surprisingly, it is also mostly legal. Yet another reason not to trust our fearless elected leaders, as if we needed that...

You, too, can aspire to become a stock market champion if you make the laws that influence the prices.

KEEP IT SIMPLE, STUPID

Sometimes, following the legislation-to-money trail is easy. Senator Tom Coburn once bought tens of thousands of dollars in bonds for a genetic technology company right around the same time he released a hold on legislation favorable to the company. He reported it per policy, so it was arguably perfectly legal. Coburn replied that the investment was made by a broker, the timing was coincidental, and the government actions couldn't be proven to increase the value of the investment. Most of us would agree that kind of potential direct impact on a market investment represents, at minimum, a conflict of interest.

IT'S GOOD TO HAVE ESP. OR FRIENDS WHO KNOW WHAT NEWS IS COMING.

Senator Dick Durbin was briefed by Treasury Secretary Hank Paulson and Federal Reserve Chairman Ben Bernanke that the economy was in deep trouble. Within 48 hours, Durbin had sold over $115K of securities, sure to be negatively impacted by a downturn. He also purchased lots of Berkshire Hathaway stock days before BH purchased a big chuck of Goldman Sachs. Savvy investing indeed.

House Financial Services Committee member Rep. Shelley Capito of West Virginia also got lucky when she coincidentally decided to dump up to a quarter million in Citigroup stock the day after the same briefing.

BUY, THEN LEGALIZE WEED...

Rep. John Yarmuth bought stock in a few cannabis companies while pushing legislation supportive of the industry. As a co-sponsor of the Marijuana Opportunity Reinvestment and Expungement (MORE) Act, Yarmuth was in a great position to influence the value of his investments. At least one of the three stocks Yarmuth purchased increased in value by a factor of nearly four, and the representative did purchase more shares in all three companies. That's sick, man...

TIMING IS EVERYTHING

Senator Reid invested somewhere between $50 and $100K in the Dow's Energy Sector Fund (IYE) in late 2005 at $29.15 per share. No problem. He later made a partial sale of IYE shares at $41.82 in August 2008. Again, no problem. One month later, Reid worked to bring a bill to the floor that would cost energy companies billions in taxes and fees. Most reasonable people would agree a bill like this would tank energy sector stock prices. The bill passed, and energy stocks, say, like IYE, collapsed 42 percent to $24.41. Good thing he sold the previous month, huh?

COVID ENRICHMENT?

Lots of elected officials made money related to the COVID pandemic. Few would argue that Capitol-dwellers had the earliest and most accurate information about both negative impacts on industry and opportunities for new businesses like treatment and vaccine companies.

Allegations have arisen linking trades on pandemic-influenced stocks by a smorgasbord of politicians, including Dianne Feinstein, Kelly Loeffler, Richard Burr, David Perdue and Rand Paul, just to name a few.

ACTIVE BIPARTISANSHIP LIVES!

While our Congress Critters can't agree on much, there is one issue where they're in lockstep—self-enrichment. According to a Washington Post report some years back, the split between Democrat and Republican lawmakers cashing in on shady market investments was almost exactly evenly split.

Regardless of party affiliation, these folks sure keep busy with stock trades. A report claims total activity for Congress in 2021 exceeded $355 million. A 2010 study determined that 150 of the 535 elected representatives in Congress exceeded congressional paycheck earnings with outside investments.

See? You, too, can make a fortune in the market in just one easy step: get elected to Congress.

If this article hasn't ticked you off quite enough, you may want to check out the book *Throw Them All Out: How Politicians and Their Friends Get Rich Off Insider Stock Tips, Land Deals, and Cronyism That Would Send the Rest of Us to Prison.*

TO BEER OR NOT TO BEER: A CONSTITUTIONAL DO-OVER

If people can be fickle, why can't entire countries be fickle, too? As it turns out, they can. We've had at least one significant about-face with a constitutional issue, meaning we added a pretty significant thing to the Constitution—the prohibition of alcohol—then just 13 years later did a complete do-over on the matter. In a loose sense, I guess the Constitution was unconstitutional for a bit.

THE 18TH CONSTITUTIONAL AMENDMENT

The 18th Amendment elevated the concept of "last call" to a whole new level.

This proposed amendment, passed by Congress in December 1917, banned the manufacture, sale, transportation, import, and export of all "intoxicating liquors" in and from the United States and its territories.

While aggressive, this amendment at least provided citizens a grace period to party like there would be no booze tomorrow. See, to make sure the process was familiar to barflies everywhere, a "last call" provision was included. Instead of 30 minutes, this one lasted for a year. The 18th Amendment was ratified by the states on January 16, 1919, thereby launching over a decade of organized crime, secret speakeasies, and plenty of moonshining, not to mention an uptight populace.

AN INTERESTING SIDE NOTE...

The United States fertility rate dropped like a depth charge during Prohibition. In fact, the rate didn't fall lower until those long gas lines of the early 1970s energy crisis. OK, there was the whole Great Depression thing, too, but it makes a much better story to assign the blame to a complete and total lack of beer.

THE 21ST CONSTITUTIONAL AMENDMENT

Prohibition? That's old news! The 21st Amendment repealed the 18th Amendment, which, as you might recall, banned the production, transport, and sale of "intoxicating liquors."

For 13 years, not one drop of alcohol was produced or consumed in the entire United States of America. Just kidding. While the drinking rates declined, people still drank like fish. Not only that, a slew of new problems like organized crime related to providing much-desired illegal "intoxicating liquors" sprouted up like Whack-a-Moles.

Eventually, Congress tired of people like Al Capone getting rich from illegal booze while the politicians lost the ability to tax it. The solution? Make alcohol legal again and stuff the federal coffers with new tax revenue.

ANOTHER INTERESTING SIDE NOTE

Drinking was never illegal during Prohibition. Remember, it was the "manufacture, sale, or transportation of intoxicating liquors" that the 18th Amendment banned. As a result, all sorts of enterprising barkeeps devised ways to dodge the law. For example, "medicinal" alcohol was still legal. Not coincidentally, all sorts of new "diseases" only treatable with alcohol sprouted up.

Oh, and have you ever heard the phrase "booze cruise?" That was another entrepreneurial victory. Customers could take a boat ride to see that invisible line in the sea that marked the edge of international waters. Since there wasn't much to see, the ship would then drive around in circles while passengers drank themselves into oblivion. The best part was that the ship's doctor didn't even have to prescribe Gin and tonics and Manhattans for seasickness—they were legal at sea.

HOW WE USED TO ELECT PRESIDENTS

If you've been baffled by the presidential election processes of each state, there's a reason for that. The original plan was a far cry from today's tsunami of direct mail flyers, television ads and kindergarten-level televised "debates." Here's how we used to elect presidents.

ELECTION BY STATE

According to Section 1 of the United States Constitution, each state can decide how to choose its electors, who collectively cast votes for the president. This was one of those compromises reached during the arguments over the Constitution itself. Some people wanted a direct popular vote. Others wanted Congress to choose the president. This whole idea of electors was intended to give each state an "equal say" in the presidential elections, even though some states are more populous than others.

TOP TWO CHOICES

As originally outlined by the Constitution, the process of picking the president was a little different than what we know today. Since electronic ballot machines had yet to be invented, each elector wrote down a vote for two individuals they thought would make swell presidents. At the state level, the votes would be tallied for all that state's electors and the sealed list was sent to the President of the Senate.

In the presence of the Senate and House of Representatives members, the Senate President opened the sealed ballot counts from each state and awarded the White House keys to the person who got a majority vote.

In the event of a tie, the House of Representatives would immediately vote to determine the winner. If no one was popular enough to obtain a majority of the electors, then the top five went into a vote by the House of Representatives. However, instead of each representative getting one vote, each state got one vote. A majority was still required, and two-thirds of states must vote.

VP: THE FIRST RUNNER UP

In this scenario, the vice president was the second-highest vote-getter. If there was a tie for second place, the Senate had to vote on the Veep pick.

Got all that? Good, because it all changed with the 12th Amendment.

With the runner-up model, it was entirely possible that the top two vote-getters were not friendly and possibly even mortal enemies, at least ideologically. In theory, the system might have created some incentive for the VP to arrange a suspicious accident in order to wear those cool Air Force One jackets. That never happened, but things did get interesting after the 1796 election when Adams, a Federalist, was saddled with Thomas Jefferson, a Democratic-Republican, as his vice president. While there were no reports of poisoned coffee, the two had some vigorous disagreements.

The 1800 election was a mess, too, but as the top two were from the same side of the aisle, there was a lengthy tie-breaking process. The net result of all this was a correction to the system outlined by the 12th Amendment. That specifies electors will cast separate votes for president and vice president. There was one other change. The eligibility requirements for vice president were made identical to those for president. The 12th Amendment was ratified on June 15, 1804.

PRESIDENTIAL SUCCESSION: THE DESIGNATED SURVIVOR

We've all seen TV and movie dramas about Presidential succession. *Designated Survivor* was a series about the Secretary of Housing and Urban Development (Kiefer Sutherland) becoming the President after a terrorist conspiracy took out the Capitol during a State of the Union address. Everyone else in the line of succession was killed in the attack, and even though (spoiler alert for the end of this article) he was number 12 on the list of succession, he won Air Force One and a beautiful home on Pennsylvania Avenue, complete with a lovely rose garden.

So, what's the real deal on Presidential Succession? Should disaster strike, what happens, and who takes charge? Our national owner's manual, the Constitution (technically a later amendment), clarifies the rules for establishing the chain of command.

THE 20TH AMENDMENT

Sections 3 and 4 of the 20th Amendment specify that Congress has the power to make laws about succession details, but they don't enumerate those details or the chain of succession.

You may have seen TV dramas that address the problem of what to do if neither the president nor vice president can perform their duties.

You may have heard that certain individuals are always stowed away in safe off-site locations during major political events like the annual State of the Union Address.

If the Capitol building fell into a giant sinkhole during the speech, the "designated survivor" would, in theory, at least be available to assume the duties of the presidency. Unless, of course, sinkholes appeared en masse. If the designated survivor doesn't survive, we're pretty sure Oprah is next in line. Just kidding. It's really Chuck Norris.

While the exact pecking order of the chain of succession is not directly written into the Constitution, the process for determining that order is. The Presidential Succession Act of 1947 outlined the current succession rules, although two prior acts did the same.

IS THE PRESIDENTIAL SUCCESSION LAW CONSTITUTIONAL?

Since Washington dwellers always have to argue about something, there is more than a bit of disagreement about whether the current presidential succession list is constitutional. Why? Primarily because congressional officials are the first two on the list! Many constitutional scholars believe they are ineligible for service in the executive branch.

That's because Article II, Section 1 of the Constitution states that only "officers" may serve as a presidential successor. Article I, Section 6 states that elected officials can't be named as "officers" of the United States during their term. Hmmm. Then again, is it really a surprise that Congress created a law to put themselves at the very top of the presidential succession hierarchy? Let's all apply our shocked faces in 3... 2... 1...

WHO'S IN CHARGE?

Ever wondered about the order of presidential succession? Here's the current ranking of designated survivors. If the priority order looks unusual, that's because cabinet positions are ranked in the order in which their respective departments came into being. That's why the Secretary of Homeland Security is last; it's the newest agency. Just to be clear, the Vice President is assumed to take charge before any of these rules come into effect.

1. Speaker of the House of Representatives
2. Senate President pro tempore
3. Secretary of State
4. Secretary of the Treasury
5. Secretary of Defense
6. Attorney General
7. Secretary of the Interior
8. Secretary of Agriculture
9. Secretary of Commerce
10. Secretary of Labor
11. Secretary of Health and Human Services
12. Secretary of Housing and Urban Development

13. Secretary of Transportation
14. Secretary of Energy
15. Secretary of Education
16. Secretary of Veterans Affairs
17. Secretary of Homeland Security

PART VIII
FOOD AND DRINK

To alcohol! The cause of, and solution to, all of life's problems.
Homer Simpson

Eating words has never given me indigestion.
Winston Churchill

A BRIEF HISTORY OF BEER

People have been drinking beer since the beginning of time. While I can't prove this in a court of law, I remain convinced brewing happy hops is the world's third-oldest profession, right after that first one and personal injury law.

BEER IS WAY OLD...

Archeologist Patrick McGovern studies remnants of old fermented joy juice by analyzing leftover traces in old pottery and such. In a nutshell, the oldest "barley beer" he's found dates back to about 3,400 BC from Iran's Zagros Mountains. Wine is older at perhaps 5,400 BC from the same area. The oldest fermented beverage he knows of is a grog from China, dating to about 7,000 BC. We're talking proof here, but many historians believe fermented beverages came on the scene about 12,000 years ago, concurrent with the development of grain agriculture.

Beer has changed a bit, and thankfully so, because the ancients found all sorts of ways to mess up perfectly good ale by adding random ingredients like olive oil, cheese, oregano, carrots, other veggies of all types and, for really wild after-parties, hemp and poppy.

LIQUID LUNCH (OR BREAKFAST)

Years ago, I received a subscription to a Beer of the Month club as a birthday gift. Like clockwork, a six-pack each of two different microbrews would arrive via the Brown Truck of Happiness. One fateful and tragic day, a "pumpkin ale" arrived, and no, it's apparently not illegal to insult, debase and torture perfectly good beer. It should be, but I digress.

The point of the story is that for a long, long time, beer wasn't a party drink, and often not very strong. Think of historical beer more as a convenient way to consume at least some healthy vitamins sourced from veggies and such. So, weird stuff (as judged by modern-day standards) like pumpkin was an integral part of beer. Wow, I coulda had a V-8 (beer)!

Poor folks, like Tom Builder, the star character of the truly fabulous book series *Pillars of the Earth* by Ken Follett, usually crammed down a hunk of bread and some "beer" to start their day. Beer was also a popular foodstuff for sailors, who constantly fought nutritional deficiencies on long voyages away from fresh foods.

AVERAGE JOE'S DRINK OF CHOICE

Some things never change. Hoity-toity cultures like the Greek and Roman civilizations preferred wine, so beer was considered the "barbarian" beverage. I guess that explains the drink of choice in modern sports stadiums, doesn't it? Anyway, back then, the Germans were considered the "barbarians," so much of the advanced development of what we'd consider good beer originated there.

While the Germans refined beer, the "make you tipsy" version was astonishingly popular in ancient Mesopotamia. You can find lots of references to deities getting tanked on beer and spilling all manner of secrets to lowly humans.

During the Babylonian empire, beer was so important that it was rationed to citizens at the rate of two liters per day for laborers and five for priests and government officials, according to the Code of Hammurabi. Some things never change. Oh, and they invented straws, too, as a way to avoid drinking the sour sludge that inevitably settled in the bottom. Word has it there was nasty stuff floating on the surface, too.

THE GOLDEN AGE OF BEER

People got serious about making what we now consider good beer in the Middle Ages, but things really took off when the monks got involved. In fact, the Kulmbacher Monchshof Kloster monastery, founded in 1349, is still making its beer. It was during this era that hops became an integral part of beer making. Thank you, monks!

Not only were monasteries centers of learning and knowledge, leading to experimenting with ingredients and brewing techniques, but they were the travel centers of their day. Travelers of all societal strata would stop over at a monastery, have a beer or three, and continue on their way. So spreadeth the joys of beer to the modern world.

We can thank the Duke of Bavaria for clamping down on adding all those nasty ingredients (like pumpkin) to beer. His beer purity decree in 1516 limited ingredients to water, hops and barley.

BEER'S PLACE IN THE WORLD

It depends on you who ask, but beer seems to occupy 4th place in most polls of the most consumed beverages worldwide, right after water, tea and coffee.

I'm betting it was in a solid second place until some idiot decided to put pumpkin in it.

WHOSE IDEA WAS IT TO DRINK COW MILK?

I'm having trouble picturing this scenario. Some ancient farmer is standing in his field, thinking, "Wow, that's one fine-looking bovine over there. Why don't we drink its bodily fluids?"

So, how and when did humans start drinking cow milk? It hasn't always been available in sterile grocery store cartons, so somewhere along the line, someone tried drinking it from the source for the first time.

We take a lot of things for granted, but once in a while, if you step back and consider what we do from a fresh perspective, you have to wonder. You know, like leaving perfectly good cheese to sit out until it gets moldy and nasty, then jacking the price and calling it Roquefort. Drinking cow milk is one of those things that seems perfectly normal now, but you have to admit, the first person to try it was either desperate or a true culinary thrill seeker.

A VERY OLD THIRSTY FARMER

Molesting cows for their half-and-half has been going on for a very long time. Contrary to some beliefs, there's evidence of the practice not just in Europe but in other regions, including Africa, Asia, and the Middle East, and early signs exist simultaneously in all those places. So, drinking cow milk didn't necessarily start in Europe. It just as likely originated in Africa, where folks have herded cows, sheep and goats for at least 8,000 years, give or take.

By examining pottery shards and... teeth from ancient skeletons, scientists have found traces of animal dairy storage in ancient kitchen containers, suggesting common consumption. The real proof lies in traces of animal dairy proteins in teeth gunk scraped from six to nine-thousand-year-old skeletons. Yup, they drank cow milk, goat milk and sheep milk.

COW MILK: AREN'T WE LACTOSE INTOLERANT?

"Were" might be the better way to classify our lactose intolerance tendencies. Six thousand years ago, almost all humans were lactose intolerant. Today, somewhere around 95 percent of all people carry the gene permitting the production of the enzyme lactase, which breaks down the lactose milk sugar.

You read the preceding dates correctly. The evidence suggests people started drinking milk while they were largely lactose intolerant. I guess when there were no grocery stores on every corner, and basic avoidance of starvation was not a given, people didn't worry too much about bellyaches and embarrassing gas expulsions at social events.

The current thinking is that, yes, people did start to drink milk before it was easy, and over a few thousand years, they developed the biological means to deal with its digestion.

So, what happened?

A WALKING NUTRITION AND HYDRATION SUPPLY

Imagine yourself living in the wild, trying desperately to scrape together enough food and pure water to keep your family and community alive. Then, one day, some super-smart guy figures out that the cows, sheep, or goats are literally walking supplies of purified water with lots of nutrition to boot. As long as one kept the animals alive and healthy, you had a daily fresh supply of part of the food and drink you required. Sure, ancient beer filled some of those needs, too, but beer tastes awful on Count Chocula.

As for the inconvenience of suffering poor digestion from lactose intolerance, that's far preferable to dying, right? So now, imagine tough times of famine, drought and disease. If you're weak, sick and lactose intolerant to boot, those "minor" symptoms suddenly become a much bigger deal, and not being able to drink a readily available source of nutrition puts you at a severe disadvantage. People who had the genetic code to thrive on an animal milk diet were more likely to prosper and grow. Next thing you know (a few thousand years), most of us can now drink animal milk comfortably.

The next time you stir up a Nestlé Quik, offer up a hat tip to that nine-thousand-year-old guy who dared to sample the bovine wares.

SPITTING FIRE... HOW TO CREATE YOUR OWN MOUTH LIGHTNING

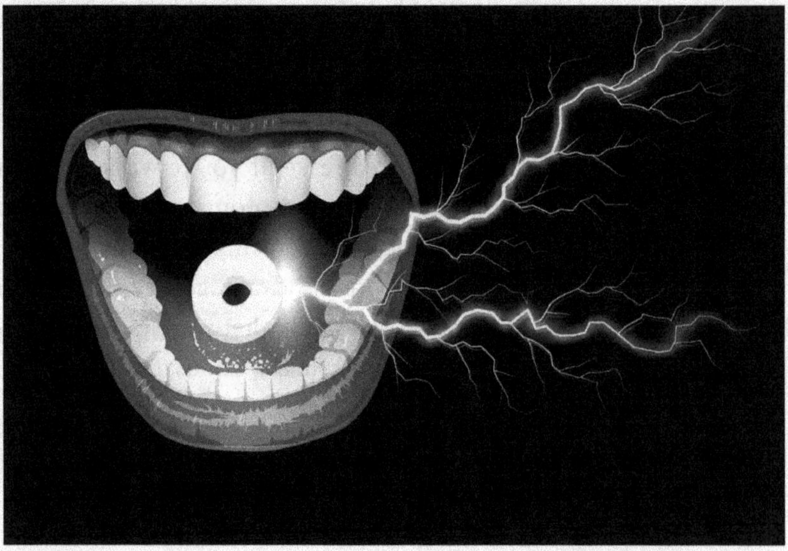

On more occasions than I'd like to remember, my mom used to spit fire. Somehow, coincidentally, I'm sure, that only seemed to happen when I got myself into trouble. Nowadays, "spitting fire" has a slightly different meaning.

The nature of fire-spitting we're going to explore today would actually pair exceptionally well with freestyle rapping if we could figure out a way to amp up the visible light energy for improved viewing pleasure.

Ever heard that legend about Wint O Green Life Savers candy? If you chomp down on that particular flavor, it results in a bit of blue/green mouth lightning. Yes, for real. Some "wives' tales" are, in fact, true.

Here's the deal.

TRIBOLUMINESCENCE

It's all about triboluminescence—the process of a substance emitting visible or invisible light when smashed, crunched or torn. Other substances exhibit vaguely similar phenomena like piezoluminescence (emitting light when deformed) or mechanoluminescence (light is emitted on exposure to a mechanical force.)

The process of triboluminescence looks something like this. Crushing these crystalline sugars knocks some electrons out of their orbit, which then proceed to smash into nitrogen molecules in the air.

As a side note, the air we breathe while munching breath mints is about 78 percent nitrogen. So, each munched electron will encounter 78 nitrogen molecules for every 21 oxygen ones. That creates a probable forecast of mouth lightning strikes. The resulting collision imparts extra energy to the nitrogen molecule. Wanting to shed this electron buzz, the nitrogen molecule emits light to return to its normal "hanging out in the air" state. If enough of this chomping and colliding happens, we see light.

NOT JUST WINT O GREEN

Many hard, sugary candies exhibit triboluminescence. It just so happens that the light output is weak and sometimes outside of the visible spectrum, depending on the nature of the sugars, so you have to work at seeing your molar power generation results. Hmm, will "molar power" catch on?

In the case of Wint O Green Life Savers, the flavor itself makes the difference. Wintergreen flavor is derived from the oil of wintergreen, or as we all know, methyl salicylate. This particular substance not only produces the triboluminescence effect; its very nature is fluorescent—it absorbs light of shorter wavelength and emits light of longer wavelength, more of which is visible to the human eyeball. In the case of Wint O Green, we see greenish-blueish light. Cool.

So, next time you're challenged to a freestyle rap battle, stuff your mouth full of Wint O Green Life Savers and get ready to spit some fire.

DO HANGOVERS GET WORSE AS YOU GET OLDER?

Yes. Hangovers get worse as you get older. You're welcome.

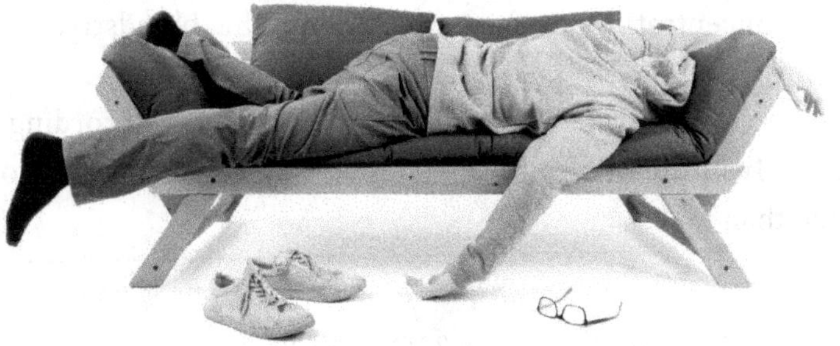

No one likes a hangover, but you'll hate them even more as you age. It's true. Hangovers get worse as you get older.

The classic wisdom says that hangovers are largely the result of dehydration and irritation of the stomach lining. That's true, but there's more detail to it than that.

As you drink, your body metabolizes your beverages somewhere at the rate of one drink per hour. Of course, that depends on how heavy a hand you use to pour and your particular body.

As you imbibe, your liver does a two-stage breakdown of all the alcohol in all those White Claws. The first stage breaks the alcohol down into acetaldehyde, which is nasty stuff. It's orders of magnitude more toxic than the alcohol itself. Stage two converts that into a non-toxic stuff called acetate. Hold this thought for a minute...

CHEAP DATES

We're not sure if this is a detriment or benefit, but the same intake of alcohol will generally have more "tipsy" effect on an older person than a younger one. As you age, your body metabolizes the booze more slowly, so it builds up and stays in your system longer.

Then, there's the body mass issue. Older folks have less water in their system. The simple reason for this is while, in our youthful era, we often have more muscle than fat, that ratio tends to flip-flop as we age. More fat than muscle means less water in the body. Ipso factor e. Pluribus Unum, less water with the same level of alcohol means a higher concentration of Jaegermeister in the bloodstream. You're drunk by 7 pm.

There's some even worse news for the ladies. According to the National Institute of Health, aging effects from alcohol are worse for women than men.

SORRY, BUT YOU'RE DETERIORATING

Age certainly correlates with lower muscle and body mass, but there's more. Consider the long list of stuff that just doesn't work as well as it used to. Reflexes, your brain, and, well, pretty much everything. Add the higher probability of a new list of daily prescription medications to treat chronic illnesses, and you end up with the following result: drinking just isn't as much fun as it used to be.

TOLERANCE

While there are plenty of exceptions (we're looking at you, Ron White), most of us tend to drink less frequently as we get older. While biology is biology and alcohol has the same effects, there is a "tolerance" factor—we learn to handle the effects of alcohol with more practice, so to speak. As we age, the frequency of funneling beer generally decreases, so say buh-bye to any developed tolerance benefits.

Just to be clear, tolerance doesn't mean you're not impaired. It simply means your body is accustomed to being drunk. Don't drive.

EVEN LOUSIER SLEEP

Pop quiz! What percentage of older people (let's call that any age over 40 for this discussion's sake) complain about not sleeping as well as they used to? Can we agree on 100 percent?

Add to the inherent lower quality of sleep alcohol's effects of making you tired but at the same time preventing your body from reaching really deep and restful sleep, and you've got a double whammy. You sleep worse before you drink, which then makes you sleep like Bernie Madoff the night before an IRS audit.

SO, WHAT ABOUT THE HANGOVERS?

For starters, the fact that consuming alcohol hits older people harder than younger ones offers a pretty good explanation of why one feels lousy the day after just a couple of drinks.

However, the real deal for the next day's senior citizen hangover blues likely comes from the combination of several issues. Hydration is even more of a challenge. Less water in the system before the shots start only makes things worse the next day. Add to that an even lousier night's sleep than you're normally getting. Last but not least, remember that acetaldehyde produced in your liver as you metabolize alcohol? Some researchers believe your body can no longer make the substance that detoxifies it as efficiently, so the half-processed toxic junk your liver manufactures makes you feel even worse. At least higher levels of acetaldehyde are linked to cancer, so in addition to monster hangovers, we have that to look forward to.

Isn't aging great?

WHAT'S THE DIFFERENCE BETWEEN ROOT BEER, BIRCH BEER AND SARSAPARILLA?

What do root beer, birch beer and sarsaparilla have in common? According to those guys selling miracle cures from the backs of wagons and 19th-century pharmacies, all of them claimed to cure whatever ails ya.

They're also delicious, and many would argue they have similar tastes. So, what is the difference between root beer, birch beer and sarsaparilla? While none of these are technically "beers," some of the originals were mildly alcoholic.

ROOT BEER CHAMPIONS

Back in my growing-up days, I have wonderful memories of excursions to the nearest A&W restaurant to get a frosty (literally) mug of root beer with a scoop or two of vanilla ice cream plunked within. A properly constructed root beer float is ecstasy. A&W was a fixture in the fast-food and treats business back in the day, at one point having more stores than McDonald's when they peaked at 2,400 or so back in the 70s.

While we're on the topic of the largest purveyor of root beer, you'd be correct if you referred to the company as Allen & Wright, as Roy Allen and Frank Wright founded the company back in 1919, expanding from a roadside stand offering—you guessed it—root beer.

FRACTIONS ARE HARD

There's another beguiling story about A&W. Back in the 80s, they took on the notorious "Quarter Pounder" by offering a better-tasting one-third-pound burger at a lower price per pound. Company executives were buying timeshares and booking cruises, confident in their plan to crush the Golden Arches before they figured out the public wasn't very good with fractions.

The burger never really took off because too many people assumed the 1/4-pound burger was bigger than the 1/3-pound burger —because, you know, four is more than three.

Besides being a likely contender for the oldest fast-food chain, some claim the company also invented the bacon cheeseburger, but that one is admittedly hard to prove. Regardless, we're glad to see A&W making somewhat of a comeback.

Now, on to the best soft drinks ever invented...

ROOT BEER

Root beer is one of those products that are named quite literally, at least in its original formulation. Even if most modern foods weren't made of plastic and other such junk, root beer would have faced a dramatic change. It was originally brewed from the Sassafras tree root and its bark. Sadly, a compound within—safrole—was deemed a likely carcinogen by the FDA back in 1960, so it's no longer used in commercial production.

Nowadays, artificial flavors are used, but that's not as bad as it sounds, as root beer is often made with a variety of other yummy spice-like ingredients, including vanilla, licorice, wintergreen, sarsaparilla (more on that later), nutmeg, cinnamon and more.

The beverage dates back to the 1700s, as far as we know, and during the 1800s, pharmacists and snake oil salesmen offered sassafras as medicinal products. In fact, one Charles Elmer Hires (sound familiar?) started selling an extract version at the 1876 Philadelphia Centennial Exposition. By 1886, he was bottling and selling it as a ready-to-consume beverage. By 1898, Barq's emerged as a serious competitor with their sarsaparilla-based version of "root beer."

BIRCH BEER

With its distinctive minty flavor, most birch beers are clear, red, and sometimes brown in color. A couple are even colored blue. Connoisseurs describe a lighter, crispier and more refreshing flavor profile when compared to traditional root beer.

Often categorized in the same general class of soft drinks, Birch beer does share some common lineage in that it's another form of "tree in a bottle." Made from boiled Birch tree bark and oils from Birch sap, this particular beverage is most popular in the northeastern US (we're looking at you, Pennsylvania) and Canada, although thankfully for us FanBoi types, it's not hard to find across the country.

Like most everything else of the era, birch beer variants found their way into 19th-century pharmacies and gained some popularity for their medicinal qualities. Early versions, and some modern ones, also packed a punch. The birch syrup would be fermented with baker's yeast to convert some of the sugars to alcohol and provide some of the distinctive fizz.

SARSAPARILLA

Sarsaparilla? I always thought it was "sasparilla." Chalk any misunderstanding up to weird pronunciation rules, kind of like "Worcestershire." Regardless of how we say it, sarsaparilla is brewed from the South American smilax ornata vine, referred to as zarzaparilla in Spanish. In other parts of the world, you might hear similar concoctions called "sarsi."

Sarsaparilla, in its true form, has a bolder flavor than root beer but tastes similar. In fact, some root beers are made using sarsaparilla instead of substitutes for the now-banned sassafras root. Just to confuse the issue, US bottlers often make sarsaparilla with birch oil instead of sarsaparilla root. Are you beginning to see the source of confusion among the three beverages?

ENJOY ONE, ENJOY ALL

These days, root beer is the sibling with an independent streak, as, in part, it is due to the death of sassafras ingredients, as the recipe varies widely between producers. You might find traces of birch and or sarsaparilla in your root beers, along with a host of other flavorings. That's not necessarily a bad thing; just be aware you might have to shop brands to find the specific recipe you prefer. Birch and sarsaparilla blends from boutique producers tend to stray less from the original formulations.

Enjoy one or all; just don't count on any of the modern blends curing a case of irritable bunion syndrome.

HOW DOES POPCORN POP?

My mom used to tell me a story about her upbringing on a farm. The primary crops were lots and lots of apples, sprinkled with a few peach and pear orchards. Her family also maintained a more limited vegetable field for fresh food for the family.

Anyway, one year, they decided to plant a sizable field of corn. Imagine their surprise when the resulting corn was... lousy. Yep, you guessed it: somehow, the desired sweet corn seeds got mixed up with the popcorn variety. Anyone need a field of popcorn? The final score? Mom and Dad: not particularly pleased. Kids: Ecstatic.

And that leads us to today's topic: how does popcorn pop?

POP HISTORY

Corn has been around 75 percent of forever, likely originating in the South and North Americas. Some pollen specimens dating back 80,000 years have been discovered with a striking similarity to what we find in today's corn. Even popcorn dates back thousands of years. Preserved ears of popcorn that are over 5,000 years old have been found.

In the 17th century, European settlers were introduced to the Native Americans' style of popcorn, cooked and popped in clay jars heated in sand. Word has it that at least some Native American tribes used the popped kernels in soup.

By the late 19th century, popcorn caught fire, pardon the pun, and became an affordable snack treat. Often served by street vendors, it made its way into movie theaters when moving pictures burst on the scene. Eventually, thanks to industry promotion, the popcorn habit arrived in the home, too. Indeed, the invention of the microwave had something to do with today's 40+-quart-per-capita consumption of blown-up fruit-veggie-grains. Yes, you read that right: corn is a whole grain, which puts it in the veggie family, but the kernel comes from the "flower," so it's also a fruit. Whatever. It's delicious.

POP VS. REGULAR CORN

You might be wondering ... is popcorn regular corn prepared differently or a different plant altogether?

While it's a member of the corn family, it's more like field or Indian Corn than the sweet corn we butter up in the summer. Four significant corn groups are Dent (field), Flint (Indian), Popcorn and Sweet. The first three have starchy kernel exteriors and are harvested after the kernels become mature and hard. Sweet corn is harvested earlier in the cycle, while the kernels are soft and yummy. That's what we normally boil and eat. If you drop Dent, Flint or Popcorn in the pot, you're guaranteed not to enjoy a lousy meal.

The primary difference between the two groups is the tougher, starchier exterior of the field, Indian and popcorn.

CULINARY EXPLOSION: HOW POPCORN POPS

By this brief explanation of the popcorn kernel, you might already be guessing how popcorn pops. The hard outer shell encloses moisture in the center of the dried kernel. When heated, the moisture turns to steam, and it begins to expand after turning to gelatinous mush. Pressure builds and eventually blows the kernel up, turning it inside out in a violent transformation.

There is some preparation involved. Tossing a freshly picked popcorn ear in a hot pan probably won't do much. Farmers and processors strip the husks and carefully dry the popcorn cobs until there's a remaining moisture level of about 14 percent. That's prime popping territory.

Then, kernels are removed from the cob, filtered to separate them from other corn junk, and polished to remove any excess material from the outside of the kernel. That's why the contents of a bag of unpopped corn look so neat and tidy.

When it arrives at your home or the neighborhood movie theater, microwaves, hot air, or a rotating hot pan raise the temperature of the kernels to around 400 degrees, and they subsequently explode, creating the basis of one of our favorite snack foods.

As for the great family farm popcorn incident? Let's just say my mom and her siblings were well-stocked for movie nights. If they'd only planted some sarsaparilla to go with...

ITCHY NUTS: WHY CASHEWS ARE ALWAYS ROASTED

Those of you blessed with the knowledge of boiled peanuts know what everyone else is missing. Roasted peanuts in the shells are delicious, too, so there is inherent culinary joy in cracking open a nut, right? But you won't see cashew nuts in their shells at your local grocery store or ballgame. So, why is that? Why can't you buy "whole" cashew nuts in their shells? And while we're at it, why are they always roasted?

ANGRY ANACARDIACEAE

The cashew tree is part of the Anacardiaceae classification of flowering plants. Even if you're not a nut lover, you're likely familiar with other Anacardiaceae family members. The group includes such delightful greenery as poison ivy, poison oak, sumac, Peruvian pepper, and, more recently, pistachio. It took some time for botanists to agree the pistachio tree was irritating enough to hang with the others.

Here's the dark family secret. Plants and trees in this family can contain urushiol. This is the oil that causes so much grief among campers, yard workers and outdoor enthusiasts of all kinds. Once urushiol has an opportunity to be absorbed into the skin, it causes that persistent rash we all know and love. Oh, and that oil sticks around for a long, long time, so contact with contaminated clothes, boots, gear, or tools can still get ya long after you leave the ivy patch.

Just to close the loop on this, cashews are part of the Anacardiaceae group. The Anacardiaceae members are usually capable of oozing urushiol from somewhere. Urushiol gives you rashes. Ipso facto e. Pluribus unum, cashews will give you a skin condition.

If you're one to enjoy cocktail nuts, you've probably noticed you haven't broken out in itchy rashes after hitting the nut bowl. Here's why...

CASHEW APPLES

Cashews grow in a kinda bizarre fashion. The nut (complete with shell) is attached to the exterior of a cashew "apple." It's kind of like Professor Quirrell in *Harry Potter,* who had an evil dark lord protruding out the back of his head. The apple is edible when fresh, but the nut presents an interesting harvesting challenge.

That urushiol is inside the shell, between the outer shell and the cashew nut itself, and it's got to go before handling and ingestion. So, cashew farmers have to exercise care when shelling the nuts, and even then, the nuts themselves are likely contaminated with urushiol after shucking.

SAVE A LIFE! ROAST YOUR NUTS, PLEASE...

OK, so I might be slightly dramatic here, but while roasting nuts may not save your life, it will avoid potential unpleasantness.

There's a reason the cashews you find in stores are always roasted. As we just discussed, raw cashews are likely to be contaminated with urushiol, and that often causes nasty and unpleasant rashes, blisters and itching. Most grocery stores agree that it's generally bad to sell food that causes such adverse effects when handled and eaten.

The good news is the heat of the roasting process destroys those urushiol oils, making cashews safe to handle and eat. Even if you do encounter "raw" cashews for sale, they've likely been cooked or similarly treated to destroy those nasty oils. Good thing. Poison ivy of the mouth would be sure to ruin your appetite.

Bon appetit!

A BIRDSEYE VIEW OF FROZEN FOOD

Those microwave burritos you buy at the gas station didn't get that way by accident. Eskimos, embezzlement, college dropouts, bankruptcy, and bugs all played a part in bringing you frozen food that doesn't taste as bad as it used to back in the day.

CLARENCE BIRDSEYE

Yep. You know the name. It's on all those boxes of frozen veggies at your local grocery store, although the Birdseye family hasn't had much to do with frozen foods since about 1938.

Birdseye was born in Brooklyn, New York, back in 1886. As a youngster, he taught himself taxidermy through mail correspondence, which apparently led him to an interest in entomology. In fact, in his two years of college, his adorable nickname was "Bugs." Clarence dropped out of Amherst after a couple of years, likely due to family financial troubles. As it turns out, his father and one of his brothers went to prison for embezzlement.

It's entirely possible that the shakeup in Birdseye's life plan caused a butterfly effect, which eventually created the frozen food aisles in your local grocery. You see, after leaving college early, Clarence ended up working for the USDA. After a couple of years, he was assigned to a post in Labrador, Newfoundland. All you really need to know about that is it can get mucho cold there, like 40-below frigid. Don't put your tongue on any streetlights.

FROZEN FISH

Not offering much in the way of sports entertainment like football or tennis, Clarence took up ice fishing, having learned the tricks from the local Inuit population.

One of those tricks was taking advantage of the blast chiller known as "outside" to freeze the fish quickly. Like cooking an egg on the hood of your AMC Gremlin in Death Valley, the opposite works, too. Waving a cod around in 40-below conditions will quickly turn it into a club.

Anyway, Clarence couldn't help but notice how yummy those fish tasted when thawed weeks or months later—much better than the mushy, cardboard sort commonly available in his hometown of New York.

SLOW FREEZING = LOUSY FOOD

Here's the thing. Traditional freezing methods of the day, done much slower than Arctic Circle processing, foster the growth of ice crystals within the cells of whatever it is you're freezing. Crystals are generally sharp, pointy things that damage soft stuff like cell walls. So, later, when the food thaws, you end up with a mushy, structure-less mess. If Jabba had frozen Han Solo in a home Frigidaire unit, he would have ended up a gooey mess like that evil Nazi in *Raiders of the Lost Ark*.

The critical takeaway is that Birdseye learned the value of flash-freezing food.

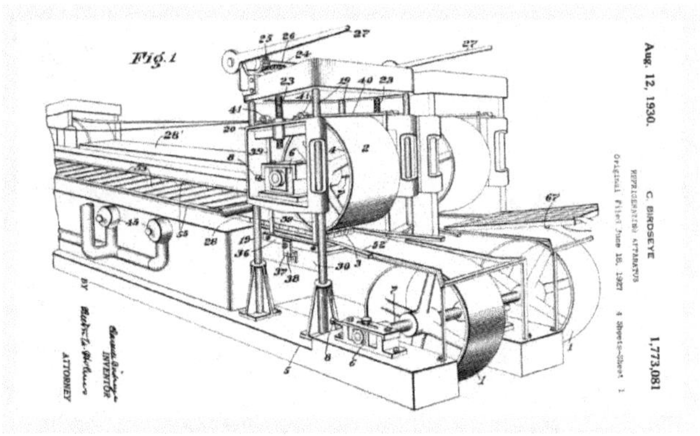

Clarence Birdseye's Flash Freezing Machine

FROZEN FOODS: TAKE ONE

Around 1922, Clarence was back in the US, tinkering with ways to freeze fish like the Inuit. After developing a method using -45-degree temperatures, he founded the Birdseye Seafoods Company. Sadly, it took the market some time to thaw to the idea of frozen foods. About two years later, the Birdseye Seafoods Company went bankrupt.

FROZEN FOODS: TAKE TWO

Not to be deterred, Clarence invented a new and improved machine, freezing packaged fish under pressure between two colder-than-ice plates. Soon after, he improved the method further, patenting a system using stainless steel belts chilled by super-cold brine.

His second company, General Seafood Corporation, was successful, and in 1929, he sold the company and his patents for a cool $22 million. That's approaching half a billion dollars today, so Birdseye's persistence paid off quite handsomely.

The next time you enjoy a 7-11 frozen burrito, save a bite in remembrance of Clarence Birdseye, won't ya?

BURNING DIRT: WHY SOME SCOTCH TASTES LIKE PEAT MOSS

Scotch whisky obtains its flavors from a variety of sources. The water used by higher-end distilleries is often a closely guarded secret used to competitive advantage. The barley used in scotch whisky production will undoubtedly have an influence, as will the handling between the germination and kilning phases. But some whisky distilleries use the old way and bring you the finest scotches by using a healthy dollop of… dirt.

Yep, that's why scotch aficionados describe some peaty varietals with words including smokey, earthy, heather, floral, seaweed, antiseptic and... iodine.

MAKING SCOTCH WHISKY

To know why varietals like Laphroaig taste like burning dirt, it's essential to know how it (and all the others in the same basic genre) is made.

While you can make "whisky" from other things like corn, wheat, oats or rye, to be a true single-malt Scotch, you must use barley as the base grain. After harvesting the prime ingredient, it's dried out, so most of the moisture (about 88%) is removed. This makes it easy to store in usable condition while still allowing germination to happen when prompted later.

Next up is the steeping step to start the malting process. After swishing the barley around in precisely controlled 16-degree Celsius water (about 60 degrees Fahrenheit), the barley is moved to drums where cool and most air encourages the germination process to start over several days. This sprouting process breaks down the barley into a form where sugars become accessible during the later mashing phase.

For this conversation, the magic happens at this next step. The germinating barley is tossed into a kiln to heat it and stop the sprouting process. Think fire and smoke. Now, hold that thought; we'll come right back to it.

To finish the process, the barley is dried, ground up and combined with heated water to make a fairly nasty liquid called wort. It's this wort, which, after cooling, is mixed with yeast to make a form of "scotch beer." Think weak barley-based alcohol, which tastes kinda foul. This lower-alcohol-by-volume mix is later distilled into the strong stuff that winds up in the bottles.

There's a lot more to those last steps, but we're here to talk about burning dirt, so we'll leave the details of the milling, mashing, fermentation and distillation processes for another story.

BURNING DIRT

Let's return to the kilning stage since we're talking about why people pay big dollars for booze that tastes like decomposing weeds.

When scotch distillers fire up that kiln to heat and dry the germinating barley, they have to use some sort of fuel for the fire, right? The highlands of Scotland aren't known for an abundance of forests and firewood, so over the centuries, folks have used dried peat moss for cooking and heating fuel. And barley kilns.

When you set that stuff on fire, most wouldn't describe the smell as anything you'd buy from Yankee Candle. It's more like burning bandaids or maybe flavored tires.

WHAT IS PEAT MOSS?

Imagine grass, weeds, shrubbery, and other assorted greenery growing across vast fields in a moist, rainy climate. Now consider its seasonal death with no one around to rake up the mess. Allow this process to repeat itself over and over for thousands of years, with new rotting vegetation dying, decomposing, and pushing down all the stuff that rotted before.

Eventually, you end up with many feet of smelly compost under the current layer of grass or whatever is native to the area. Ipso facto E. Pluribus unum, we're talking dirt. You might consider this stuff underaged coal. Locals call it peat.

As it turns out, when you're poverty-stricken, and the area where you live is light on trees for firewood, you figure out you can dig up hunks of this detritus, let them dry for a few weeks and then burn them. Mmmm. Smells delicious. Don't use it in your BBQ smoker if you want repeat guests.

Well, this is precisely what happened in Scotland way back in the days before microwave cooking. While peat isn't so much a standard heating and cooking fuel anymore, it is still used to heat those kilns to dry out malted barley. And guess where all that smoke and stink goes?

That's right, into the barley itself, giving "peaty" scotches their unique flavor.

We should note one more variable at play. Consider how different vegetation grows in the hills, plains and coastal areas. The rotting plant flesh acquires unique "flavors" depending on its flora, so different peated scotches will have different smoky flavors. Those coastal peat varietals might even acquire notes of dead fish and seaweed. Yum!

One more thing. If you're a peat-head, don't worry about running out. Somewhere over 20 percent of Scotland is covered with the stuff.

DIRTLESS SCOTCH

All scotch whisky isn't dirty. Much of what you find in the liquor store aisles is made like other spirits, relying on the characteristics of the water supply and barley for each brand's distinctive taste. But a subset of scotch distilleries treasure those childhood memories of cooking mud pies and go all out to bring you that, um, unique flavor profile peat-heads so enjoy.

I'm poking some fun here, but in all seriousness, a "peaty" scotch can be delectable.

Of course, it's an acquired taste.

RADIOACTIVE BANANAS: IT'S WHAT'S FOR BREAKFAST

I do enjoy a fresh banana for breakfast. It feels filling and satisfying and seems to offer a bit of a start-the-day boost. Perhaps that's from the sugars. Or perhaps it's the radioactivity—that seemed to work for Spider-Man, so why not us regular folks? On further thought, Curious George and King Kong seemed to do alright on a healthy intake of bananas, too. But let's not blow by that earlier statement. Come on, man, are bananas really radioactive?

RADIOACTIVITY IN A BANANA PEEL

Yeah, I know we're playing fast and loose with idioms, but to fully explore the radioactive breakfast food question, we need to understand the Cliff Notes on radioactivity. We know that people get all weird about it. Some guy named Schrodinger even used the concept of radioactivity to help postulate a cat being both alive and dead at the same time.

To describe radioactivity in a friendly way for those among us who are less durable in spirit, envision an unstable atom. As it decays, things like electrons, neutrons, alpha particles or maybe gamma rays may leave the premises and venture forth into the world. That's what radiation is.

It doesn't sound too threatening because atoms are really, really small. The problem is that these orphaned particles carry energy that can break down (ionize) other particles they encounter. When a whole bunch of tiny things all wreck untold numbers of other tiny things like falling dominoes, the situation can get hairy.

In the face of radiation exposure, we fret about things like radiation sickness, cancer and even burns. That happens when radiation destroys and alters organic molecules.

POTASSIUM IS ELEMENTAL

Sure, Mom always reminded you to eat foods like bananas and spinach to "get your potassium," so if Mom said it, we definitely needed it. And a banana has about 425 milligrams of potassium. Groups of potassium atoms always have a small sub-clique of nonconformists called K-40. Remember high school chemistry? K is the symbol for potassium. K-40 is an unstable, radioactive mutant, somewhat like that crazy aunt you dread inviting to Thanksgiving.

Anyway, K-40 is radioactive but decidedly lackadaisical in the commitment area, having a half-life of something like a billion years. Without boring the potassium out of you, hardly any radiation is emitted from a banana, at least in our lifetimes. And as we all know from experience, a fresh banana is sure to start decomposing within 12 minutes after getting home from the store.

BANANAS = INSTANT DEATH?

I know what you're thinking. This idiot just ruined my breakfast, and future table-side bananas foster dessert experiences. Will you now feel electrons blasting through your body, headed en masse for the nearest nuclear bomb factory, every time you enjoy a banana?

Nah, and the level of exposure you get from a banana is less than the odds of a Congressman reaching for the lunch tab. Barely. Because of that unimpressive half-life, a banana only emits about .01 millirems of radiation. To put that in perspective, an X-ray doses you with somewhere between a few and hundreds of millirems, depending on the type. Flying across the country will blast you with 30 or more millirems—round trip. And your granite countertop leaks 0.1 millirems per year.

So enjoy your banana daiquiri. Just don't leave it on the granite countertop too long. In a billion years or so, it just might become dangerous.

WHY DOES BACON SMELL SO GOOD?

Why is it that the smell of sizzling bacon has the power to wake one from a dead sleep? I suppose an obnoxiously bad smell, like skunk, might have the same power, but I've never tried it, and a skunk awakening is not on my bucket list.

It seems there's a never-ending supply of interesting facts about food... You might think the snap, crackle and pop sounds of frying bacon might have something to do with it, but while I can't speak for you, L'eau de Sizzling Bacon maintains its power even if you're too far away to hear it.

By the way, I think Kellogg stole the "Snap, Crackle, Pop" thing from bacon to help sell their Rice Krispies. That didn't come on the scene until 1929, and we all know folks were leaping out of bed in a dash for first in the bacon line long before that. But I digress.

What is it about bacon smell that can bring back the dead?

BACON SMELL: VOLUME RULES

The process of cooking bacon releases about 150 unique compounds that meld together, creating the bouquet we all know and love.

The compounds have all sorts of scientific and, for describing the delicious smell, useless names. Hydrocarbons, aldehydes, pyridines, pyrazines, ketones, alcohols—what's the difference? A lot, actually. These by-products of cooking meat, especially bacon, arguably have supernatural olfactory powers.

Hydrocarbons are simple things made of various combinations of hydrogen and carbon atoms. Different combinations produce different smells. Aldehydes are similar; they are constructed of hydrogen and carbon atoms but with the addition of oxygen. Pyridines and pyrazines contain nitrogen, and that's where a large part of the answer lies.

THE MAILLARD REACTION

The smell of sizzling bacon is so important that the science community uses a special term to describe the process. OK, so the Maillard Reaction isn't unique to bacon but cooking food in general. Think browning various things. Meats are usually the easiest example.

The reaction is between the sugars and amino acids, or carbohydrates and proteins if you will. Bacon has a healthy supply of sugars and fats, so its Maillard Reaction is particularly aggressive—in a polite, loving and delicious-smelling way. The by-products of the

Maillard Reaction are... all those hydrocarbons, aldehydes, pyridines, pyrazines, ketones, and alcohols.

WHY BACON?

The scent of cooking meat appeals to many regardless, but bacon has a little extra juice compared to other foods.

The salting and brining processes used in lots of bacon varieties help produce a heavier concentration of those nitrogen-containing compounds, which helps explain the more powerful fragrance of bacon over, say, a hamburger.

Are you hungry now?

HOW HOT DOGS ARE MADE: ARE THEY REALLY GROSS?

When I was a kid, we used to do an annual freezer-stocking event by butchering our own pig. The hams, bacon and other "normal" cuts were delicious, but the lowlight of the process was the making of something called "Pan Haus," pronounced, at least in Western Maryland, "Pawn Hoss." Also called PaanHaas (the Pennsylvania Dutch version), Panhas, Pawnhas and Scrapple, one might say it's made from everything in the pig except the squeal. #Truth.

Anyway, as I enjoyed today's lunch of cheese dogs with heaps of Dijon mustard, it occurred to me that hot dogs have earned, fairly or not, a reputation for being made from creative ingredients. Let's explore how hot dogs are made.

INGREDIENTS

OK, let's consider the ingredients of the hot dogs I lazy-fried for lunch today in a frying pan. I'll leave the brand name out because there's no need to disparage anyone, but let's say it's a quality brand. And come on, we all know hot dogs are made from, well, let's say, the less-refined cuts of meat or pork, so does who makes them really matter? Here goes:

Meat, water, spice, sodium lactate, paprika, hydrolyzed soy protein, garlic powder, sodium diacetate, sodium erythorbate, flavoring and sodium nitrate.

See? That doesn't sound so bad except for all the "iums" and "ates." Oh, and the second most prevalent ingredient is water. But you know there has to be more to the story, or else hot dogs wouldn't have the reputation of the land version of oysters. The secret lies in creative definitions of "beef."

HOW HOT DOGS ARE MADE

The primary ingredient of all but the very worst hot dogs is... meat. But unless the chef at Spago is making yours, the source of said meat is all the leftover "trimmings" from the more edible parts of beef, pork and chicken. See what they did there? Like my realtor calling the swamp behind my house "wetlands," the hot dog industry uses appealing marketing terms, too.

Anyway, the scraps are shoveled up (most reputable hot dog makers use different shovels for this than the ones used to clean the stalls) and tossed into a grinder to standardize the "trimmings." OK, I'm just kidding. No shovels and no stalls.

Once ground, blending in additional flavoring and texturizers like food starch, salt and other seasonings is easier. The ones I'm eating as I write have garlic, paprika and other unnamed flavorings.

Remember, the number two ingredient is water, so that, and sometimes corn syrup is pumped into the mix to help spread things around. Once well blended, the mix is squished to get the air out, prepping the "batter" for actual dog making.

Nearing the end of the process, the batter is oozed into cellulose casings and cooked. Sometimes, smoke flavor is added for taste. After cooking, the casing is peeled off before packaging since the interior dog is now somewhat solid.

YOU'RE SAFE. MOSTLY.

While "trimmings" leave room for interpretation, the days of picking up scraps from the floor are long past us. Things are highly regulated now, and "unusual" ingredients like you'd find in head cheese aren't in your common hot dogs unless the ingredients label says something like "variety meats."

That doesn't mean you're just getting the outside edge of a ribeye steak. A percentage of hot dog meat can be made from the less desirable stuff closer to bones and whatnot, but we're still not getting into gross organs or faces.

You're welcome. Now go enjoy that chili dog.

PART IX
SPACE AND OUR UNIVERSE

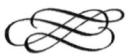

When a man sits next to a pretty girl for an hour, it seems like a minute. Let him sit on a hot stove for a minute and it's longer than any hour. That's relativity.

Albert Einstein

Two possibilities exist: either we are alone in the Universe, or we are not. Both are equally terrifying.

Arthur C. Clarke

To confine our attention to terrestrial matters would be to limit the human spirit.

Stephen Hawking

Space isn't remote at all. It's only an hour's drive away if your car could go straight upwards.

Sir Fred Hoyle, British Astronomer

WHAT DOES SPACE SMELL LIKE?

Space is a trip. Ponder how the overwhelming majority of everything is really... nothing. No air. No up or down. In the vastness of the universe, things just float around. We're so accustomed to our little ball of mass with its associated gravity that it's nearly impossible to imagine anything else as the normal state of things.

As space is a vacuum, meaning there's no air or much of anything else, we have to ask, what does space smell like? Can it even have an odor? Is there anything in it for our noses to detect?

OPENING THE WINDOW TO FIND OUT

Part of the difficulty in answering this question results from our inability to open a window and take a whiff. Sure, it's technically possible for an astronaut to do that, but that one inhale will be their last unless they're somehow able to get back inside and regenerate the air supply post haste.

With absolutely zero oxygen intake, a human would lose consciousness in about 15 seconds, give or take. Thinking of taking a deep breath before opening the door? Don't do that either. Let's keep the gore out of this and say the air in your system would expand, causing damage to your lungs, and various stuff inside you would start to boil.

If the short-term effects of space exposure aren't harmful enough, you also have to worry about micrometeorites (pretty unlikely) and radiation effects. Oh, and it's cold, something like minus 250 degrees Fahrenheit.

Bottom line? We can't take a whiff of space to learn what it smells like.

THE SPACE MUDROOM

However, Astronauts have provided some insight into the "what does space smell like" question. After playing outdoors, they eventually have to get back into the house via the space mudroom, which engineers call an airlock.

So, picture the scenario where an astronaut or two comes back from space into an airlock and then hits the "pressurize" button, introducing some semblance of a normal, breathable atmosphere into the airlock. When that process is complete, they can remove the helmet and take a whiff. And, of course, when they open the door between the airlock and the rest of the ship or station, other astronauts inside get a sampling of whatever odors they brought in.

SMELLS LIKE...

Many astronauts have described the unique smell of space. Keep in mind they're describing the smell of our solar system. Other systems and galaxies have entirely different smells, ranging from delicious berries to rotten eggs—and everything in between.

As for the closer-to-home odors, most spacewalkers describe a burning smell, usually like a burnt metal. Astronaut Don Pettit spent summers during his youth doing lots of welding while repairing large machinery. He describes the space scent in terms similar to freshly welded metal.

Others liken our space to charcoal grills, burnt meat and ozone. Of course, we all have unique sniffing abilities and detect and describe scents differently, but the "burnt" descriptor comes up nearly every time.

GENERATED SMELLS?

One possibility for at least some of the smell is minor chemical reactions occurring when the spacewalker brings in "debris" from outside in the form of molecules and atoms stuck to their suits, helmets and equipment.

While space is mostly a vacuum, that doesn't mean there aren't lots of particles floating around for eternity. For example, loose oxygen atoms may come in with the space traveler and, once inside, combine to form 02. Or, perhaps UV rays split O2 in the station or suit environments into single oxygen atoms, and they end up forming ozone.

THE SMELL OF DEATH

Another source of space aroma is dead stars.

Polycyclic aromatic hydrocarbons aren't limited to the cosmic universe. This stinky stuff in some foods and other natural compounds exists here on Earth, too. We also create it when burning things like wood, tobacco and meat. Are you seeing a connection?

Anyway, one significant source of polycyclic aromatic hydrocarbons is dying stars. When a star kicks the bucket, it doesn't just fade out like a candle at the bottom of its wick. It's a certified conflagration that scatters stuff into space with violent abandon. And remember, space is a near vacuum with no resistance, so things travel more or less forever. Eventually, we'll catch it and smell it here in our own solar system.

Anyway, there you have it. The next time a restaurant server anxiously awaits my evaluation of a freshly opened bottle of wine, I'm going to say, "Mmm! This one has notes of space!"

FIXING A SERIOUSLY EXPENSIVE MIRROR: THE HUBBLE SPACE TELESCOPE

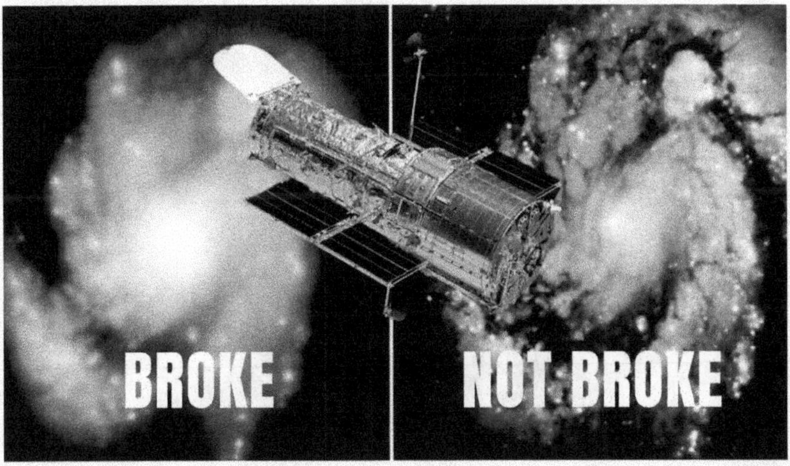

If breaking your $11 shaving mirror causes seven years of bad luck, what happens when you mess up a $2 billion dollar one?

The Hubble space telescope was designed to show us, in exquisite detail, the farthest reaches of the galaxy. There was one slight problem. It didn't work because it was technically "broken." OK, not in the traditional sense of a big crack or shattered glass, but a small manufacturing defect causing distant images to be blurrier than expected.

Sure, it was still far better than earth-bound telescopes, but when you're spending $2 billion, things better be perfect.

BIG BUCKS: THE HUBBLE SPACE TELESCOPE MIRROR

The main mirror of the Hubble space telescope is a whopper, weighing in at 1,825 pounds thanks to its 7.8-foot diameter main mirror. Imagine trying to hang that on your wall. Its purpose is to collect lots of dim light and reflect it back to a much smaller 12-inch mirror, from which point the image is collected, processed and sent back to Earth.

It took about eight years to build, but it had to wait a few extra years until its April 24, 1990 launch, owing to the 1986 Challenger disaster, which delayed the space program by years. By the time the Hubble was ready to report to work, the price tag approached a cool $2 billion. A life-cycle accounting might put the total price tag closer to $12 billion since an additional 10 (ultra) large were sunk into subsequent maintenance missions.

The Hubble main mirror with its 1/50th of a hair flaw. Can you see it?
Image: NASA

A FRACTION OF A HAIR

When you're manufacturing a multi-billion dollar deep space telescope, details matter. After the Hubble telescope was yeeted into space, scientists were a bit puzzled at the lower-than-expected image quality of cosmically far away stuff.

Upon further investigation, it turned out that the primary mirror manufactured back in 1979 (remember Hubble was launched in 1990) had a tiny, tiny defect.

The edge of the mirror has a slight discrepancy caused by the miscalibration of polishing equipment. The difference between the actual and design specs was only 1/50th the width of a human hair, but that was enough to cause major distortion when peeking at stuff billions of light-years distant.

SPACE GLASSES

Since the cosmos doesn't have a warranty return program, engineers had to figure out a solution. While the Hubble was never designed for an easy main mirror swap, it was designed for future maintenance missions to keep it in tip-top shape—at least for planned improvements and fixes of old or worn components.

In fact, there have been five service calls to the Hubble space telescope between 1993 and 2009. Next time you gripe about a $125 minimum charge for the plumber to come take a look, consider each space shuttle launch cost $1.5 billion, so those service calls were pricey.

Clever engineers figured out a way to avoid replacing the main mirror by making a sophisticated pair of "glasses" to correct its vision. It's kind of like figuring out a corrective lens prescription for a nearsighted person rather than replacing their eyeballs.

Anyway, two gadgets were installed to fix Hubble's eyesight: the Wide Field and Planetary Camera 2 (WFPC2) and the Corrective Optics Space Telescope Axial Replacement (COSTAR). The COSTAR system, designed by Ball Aerospace, consists of five pairs of small mirrors mounted on moveable articulated arms, which corrected the fault in the light beam from the defective main mirror.

See? Space glasses.

WHAT ALIENS LEARN FROM SATELLITE TV

As I write this, the Tau Cetites are enjoying their first decade of watching the *Power Rangers.* In the interest of learning, Tau Ceti is about 11.9 light-years from Earth. While that's "reach out and touch someone" close in terms of cosmic distances, it's not even the closest star we know of with planets and the possibility of alien life. That would be Proxima Centauri b, which is about 4.24 light-years from any of our TV broadcast facilities.

On a related note, I'd like to take this opportunity to apologize on behalf of all earthlings to citizens of the two potentially habitable planets there for sending *Power Rangers* their way.

Thinking about ET watching DirecTV from Earth is an interesting idea, although somewhat of a fantasy. Since most TV viewers actually live on Earth, signals aren't optimized for deep-space transmission. They're broadcast spherically, and if there's any aiming done, it's in the direction of the horizon. The problem is that any signals that do escape Earth become billions and billions of times weaker on the way to our interstellar neighbors. So, by the time *Keeping Up with the Kardashians* makes it to Proxima Centauri b, it's coming across as unintelligible background noise devoid of meaning. You know, just like here on earth.

If there is alien life somewhere in the expanse, perhaps we can assume they have superior satellite dish technology that can pick up our nightly TV anyway. I'd even bet they can unscramble the premium channels and avoid paying the $9.99 monthly access. It's good to be an advanced alien life form.

So, what would they learn? That question got me thinking. If some intelligent life form is out there, and they watched a few hours of prime-time television, they might reach some interesting conclusions about life here on Earth.

- Most humans have diseases that can only be treated using drugs with ridiculous names.
- The most perfect of human specimens work at Wal-Mart stores and McDonalds.
- When a human is ready to marry, a dozen members of the opposite sex join them at an all-expense-paid luxury resort where their prospective spouses grovel for affection while spreading rumors that their peers are whores.

- To own a car, one must correctly guess "Before and After" phrases, even though some letters are missing.
- Everyone has their own personal Personal Injury Attorney.
- Sharks kill 67% of all humans annually.
- Lunch ladies spike the Turkey Tetrazzini with PCP. It's the only explanation for human behavior as portrayed on C-SPAN and cable news talk shows.
- It's illegal to talk loudly during golf.
- Pundits with the least amount of relevant experience claim to have all the great ideas.
- Everyone is murdered at least once daily.
- Mickey Mouse Club membership is a shortcut to future sex and drug scandals.
- Wars are fought between cities by groups of grossly overpaid and egomaniac mercenaries dressed in skintight yet colorful uniforms. Losing cities have to buy the beer and lobsters.
- The residents of Hollywood earn their living by giving awards to each other when they're not recovering from plastic surgery.
- Humans who are particularly annoying and like to dress in skimpy clothes are banished to tropical islands where they are forced to eat bugs and tarnish each other's reputations while saying they're being honest and loyal.
- The most successful earthlings drink beer continuously while wearing exotic fragrances.
- Those who should probably be in charge of earth's government compete nightly over trivia. Those with trivial brains compete daily for microphone time in front of the Capitol.

Did I miss anything?

THE MOON LANDING CONSPIRACY... CONSPIRACY

People love a good conspiracy theory. A 1999 Gallup poll reported that six percent of people believed that the moon landings were fake. An additional five percent indicated they were still undecided about the "moon landing conspiracy."

MOON LANDING CONSPIRACY CLAIMS

The explanations surrounding the persistence of the "NASA faked the moon landings" claims include some pretty creative reasoning.

- It's impossible for people to walk on the moon because it is made of light.
- The landings were filmed on a sound stage either somewhere in the Hollywood Hills or hidden within Area 51 with the aid of *2001: A Space Odyssey* filmmaker Stanley Kubrick.
- When Buzz Aldrin planted the flag, it moved as if it were being moved by wind. That's impossible in the vacuum of space.
- All those micrometeorites that have been bombarding the moon for eons would have instantly perforated Neil and Buzz. Besides, they would have died from exposure to the Van Allen radiation belt on the way there.
- Camera lens crosshairs etched onto the glass were covered by astronauts and other objects in the photos. Unpossible!
- Stars aren't visible in the photos.
- Where's the blast crater underneath the lunar lander?
- Shadows of various objects in the same photo frame aren't parallel.

The list goes on, with the most egregious being that the Apollo 1 launch pad fire that killed Command Pilot Gus Grissom, Senior Pilot Ed White, and Pilot Roger B. Chaffee was a government-sponsored hit aimed at stopping the trio from going public with the fakery.

THE MOON LANDING CONSPIRACY BEGINS

The moon landing conspiracy arguably started, or at least gained steam with the release of the book *We Never Went to the Moon* by Bill Kaysing, a technical presentations specialist with Rocketdyne Propulsion Field Laboratory from 1956 to 1963. Kaysing claimed the role of insider whistleblower on the moon landing being a made-up hoax. The gist was that NASA was capable of putting ships and astronauts in orbit but not landing them on the moon. Massive pressure to "beat the Russians" supposedly led to an elaborate fakery of the actual moon landings.

APOLLO MOON LANDING CONSPIRACY... DEBUNKED

While we can't spend the next week going through all the details of debunking, we can touch on some of the highlights.

As for the "moon is made of light" thing, I suppose someone ought to alert the tides that the moon isn't really moving them around.

Approximately 600 million people watched the moon landings on live television. I love the movie *2001: A Space Odyssey* as much as the next geek, but come on, man, the special effects aren't exactly compelling enough to fool a TV audience of hundreds of millions.

Where are all the stars? Image: NASA

No stars? The photos from the moon landings were taken in lunar daylight. While the sky is black, stars aren't going to be highly visible to a camera with a necessarily small aperture setting for those bright and reflective lunar surface conditions.

Fake shadows!!! Image: NASA

Non-parallel shadows? It's called perspective. You can replicate this effect yourself when the sun is low in the sky. Many of the lunar landing conspiracy theories don't properly account for ginormous environmental differences between the Earth and the moon, like vacuum conditions, low gravity, complete lack of dust or haze in the air and the myriad of highly reflective surfaces present.

As for the flag? Well, Buzz was rocking the flag to plant the pole in the lunar dirt. And the flag was designed with a horizontal support bar inside the top seam of the flag itself. A week or so of being stuffed into a tube, combined with incomplete extension of the support rod, and... voila! Ripples in the flag material, but no movement from the non-existent lunar wind.

And the list of debunked myths goes on and on. In 2009, a lunar reconnaissance orbiter mapped the moon using cameras with orders of magnitude improved resolution. Guess what? The landing sites are all there in plain view. With no wind or rain, those footprints will be around for 75 percent of forever. And, of course, there are the 838 pounds of lunar rocks returned to Earth, which have subsequently been examined by thousands of scientists around the world. They're real. Even France agrees.

But to me, the biggest debunker in the schoolyard is human nature itself. Somewhere over 400,000 people were involved in the space program. Isn't it weird that at least some haven't spilled the beans in the past 50+ years? You know what they say. Three people can keep a secret—if two of them are dead.

While few dispute Saturn V rockets took off from the Florida coast, many don't believe we actually completed the finale of a moon landing. There's a fascinating book, *Moon Lander: How We Developed the Apollo Lunar Module,* by Chief Engineer Tom Kelly. He ran the Grumman development program, where some 7,000 employees, including 3,000 engineers, designed and built the lunar landers. It's a great read for a rainy day.

That's a lot of people doing a lot of fake work for a lot of fake years for a fake machine designed to perform a fake moon landing.

THE NORTH STAR, SPINNING TOPS AND OUR MIND-BENDING UNIVERSE

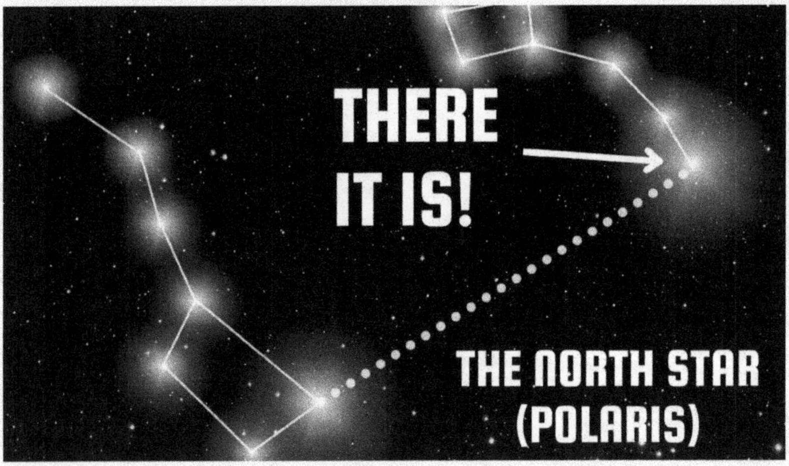

Look up. How many stars do you see? If you had unobstructed vision around the earth in all directions, and if we didn't have an atmosphere to cloud up the view, you'd see, in theory, at least 200 billion trillion stars. If I don't miss any zeroes, that's 200,000,000,000,000,000,000,000. That's almost as much as our politicians could spend in a year if they put their minds to it.

And that doesn't begin to count planets. In our solar system, we have eight, or maybe nine, depending on Pluto's current membership status. But who knows how many planets all those stars have circling them like starving paparazzi? And don't get me started on moons. The net-net is that there is a whole bunch of stuff in the universe.

If you want to break your brain, consider more than a few astrophysicists believe that at the moment before the Big Bang, all the matter in the known universe, those 20 sextillion stars and all of their associated groupies, were compressed into a space one-trillionth the size of the period at the end of this sentence. Sorry, not sorry for plunging your gray matter into the abyss of "mind blown" for the day.

INFINITY IN MOTION

The cool thing to see is all the motion of our little slice of that vast universe. If you put down the smartphone, go outside, and chill out for a couple of hours while looking to the heavens, you'll see all those stars and constellations we've named moving around the sky. It's fascinating.

Actually, what we see isn't the universe moving but the earth spinning. Sure, the universe *is* expanding. Back in the 1920s, Edwin Hubble (yeah, the guy the telescope is named after) figured out the universe is expanding, and the outermost reaches of the universe are expanding at a faster rate than the inner billions of trillions of stars. His work inspired the Hubble Constant, which, when multiplied by a galaxy's distance, can begin to describe these relative velocities. Some smart folks, but not all, believe the math works out to somewhere around 70 km per second per Megaparsec distance.

In case you're wondering, a Megaparsec is about 3.26 million light years. That's a long way, far beyond the range of today's most exotic electric cars. To put the distance in perspective, Proxima Centauri b, the closest star with planets, is about 4.24 light years from here.

OUR SPINNING TOP

But back to more comprehensible things and how you can use some of this mind-bending information.

All those stars appear to move in the sky because we spin around our polar axis like a top. So, if you left your camera on all night pointed up, you'd see a circular pattern of star movement.

If you're reading this from the Galápagos Islands, you're zipping along right now at about 1,037 miles per hour thanks to the earth's rotation. Of course, if you live closer to one of the poles, you're moving much slower, say about 500 mph in Anchorage, Alaska. And if you're standing on Santa's barber pole, you're not moving at all but perhaps getting dizzy from spinning in place. OK, the spinning sensation part isn't true, but you have to admit it makes for a great visual.

NORTH STAR TIPS AND TRICKS

All of this spacey stuff does have some practical application.

I always get a kick out of finding the North Star. Serious astronomers call it Polaris, perhaps because it is positioned over the North Pole and not subject to moving around the sky like all the other stars. That makes it a wonderful navigation aid, at least at night, provided you can find it. Assuming you're in the northern hemisphere and it's a clear night, you can get a pretty decent fix on which direction is up.

THE BIG DIPPER POINTS THE WAY

Finding Polaris (the North Star) is easy if you've ever spotted the Big Dipper. Didn't we all do that as kids?

Just look for the "dipper" part, not the handle, and follow the two stars that define the side of the cup away from the handle, and they point right to Polaris.

It's a fun trick to file away and share when enjoying the outdoors at night. Who knows? That knowledge might save your life or, at minimum, help you get your bearings when in a new place.

NORTH STAR…FOR NOW

Now for the bad news. If you live to the ripe old age of 15,000 or so, you won't be able to use the North Star for navigation anymore. Remember the spinning top thing? Earth wobbles like a toy top but far more slowly.

Thanks to this precession (the scientific term for wobbling), the star Vega will be the new North Star. No worries, though; by 27,000 AD or so, Polaris will be back in charge and pointing the way north again.

HOW MANY ATOMS FIT ON THE HEAD OF A PIN?

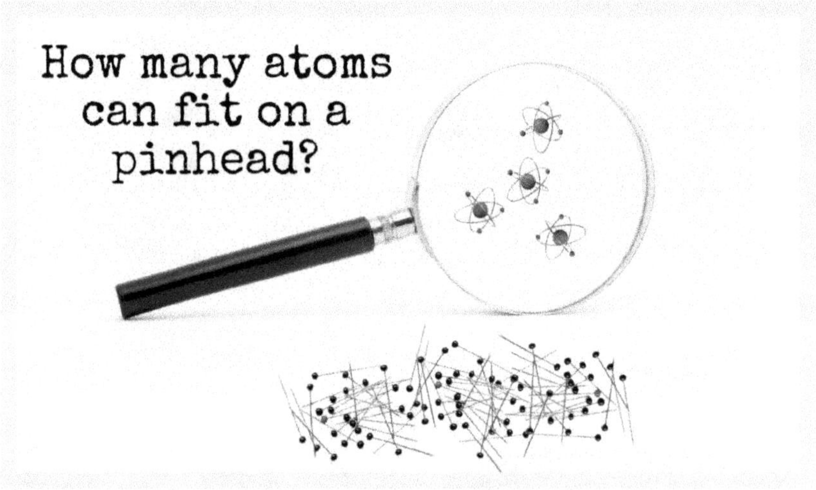

After all this time, we still don't know exactly what stuff is made from or precisely how gravity works. This whole debate about "settled science?" Ha!

We know things are made from molecules, and molecules are made from atoms. The next level is pretty "settled," too; atoms are made from protons, electrons, and neutrons. But what are they made from? Scraggly-haired physicists talk about quarks and the gluons holding them together. The Standard Model says quarks are fundamental particles, not made of anything smaller. But science marches on, so who knows? Plenty of smart people are talking about subcomponents of quarks.

Anyway, before migraines set in, just how big are atoms? And more importantly, how many atoms fit on the head of a pin?

SQUISHY MEASUREMENT APPROXIMATIONS

The head of a pin is easy to measure. Being solid, at least at the scale we see and touch, we can stick calipers across it and come up with a diameter somewhere in the neighborhood of a millimeter, depending on your particular tastes in pins.

Atoms, on the other hand, are more like measuring our solar system. There are no hard edges, nor do we have calipers small enough. The simple Hydrogen atom has a proton in the middle and an electron in orbit, so we need to measure the orbital diameter.

To visualize the scale of the proton and electron, think of the center of a Hydrogen atom as a pea (the garden variety) and the orbital space as a large football stadium. Plop the pea on the 50-yard line, and the electron orbits around the upper deck. That's what our Hydrogen atom looks like in itty-bitty scale. Even with its "solar system" measurement, a Hydrogen atom is just about .1 nanometers in diameter. That's .1 billionths of a meter.

That's just Hydrogen. Other atoms are different sizes and have different weights. For example, an Oxygen atom has eight protons, eight electrons and eight neutrons, so it's somewhat larger.

SO, HOW MANY ATOMS FIT ON THE HEAD OF A PIN?

We'll use round numbers as this stuff gets hairy. Let's assume a pinhead is 1 millimeter across. Doing the old geometry math, it should have a surface area of about 0.000000007853975 meters.

Now for the Hydrogen atom. Since it's a "ball," we have to slice it in half and measure the cut surface area to get an idea of how many can rest on the pinhead or else they'll just roll off while we're counting. That "half" is about 0.0000000000000000007853975 meters. If you do the long division, carry the one, and all that, we're estimating 1,000,000,000,000 will fit on the pinhead. What a handy number to memorize, huh? Like your old math teacher said, "You'll use that one day!"

HOW MANY ATOMS DO YOU HAVE?

We've figured out atoms vary in size depending on their type, so we have to consider what type of atoms make up the average human body. Most people consist almost entirely of Hydrogen, Oxygen, and Carbon, although I maintain a higher percentage of Reese's Peanut Butter Cups atoms than average folk. Those first three atom types represent about 99 percent of our mass. But I digress.

Given the balance of these three elements, we can calculate the number of atoms we've got hanging around our midsection and the rest as follows. We're about 2/3 Hydrogen, 1/4 Oxygen and 1/10 Carbon. I'll spare you the math of figuring out the relative size of each of those percentages and offer up the answer directly.

7,000,000,000,000,000,000,000,000,000

If I'm counting all those 27 zeroes correctly, you can also say that as seven billion, billion, billion. If each atom represented one dollar, that's almost as much money as politicians have bamboozled in the past 250 years.

DOES THE MOON HAVE AN ATMOSPHERE?

True or false: The moon has an atmosphere.

Well, what's your answer?

If you said "yes," you're technically correct. Sort of.

LAMEST ATMOSPHERE EVER?

The moon's atmosphere is really, really thin, so thin that, in fact, it doesn't even provide any insulation as does Earth's. That's one of the reasons the temperature range is so darn uncomfortable on the moon. It ranges from about 260 degrees Fahrenheit in the direct sun to -279 degrees Fahrenheit when it's dark. Definitely wool coat weather, but you'll have to leave it at home when the sun comes out and break out the Speedo with plenty of sunscreen.

WHAT'S IN THE "AIR?"

I'm using "air" somewhat loosely because there isn't any. Technically, the moon's atmosphere is an exosphere. That's a nebulous and boundaryless region with a breathtakingly low density of whatever is in it. In terms of density, it's somewhat similar to Earth's exosphere, which is about 300 miles above us.

In the moon's exosphere, there is helium, argon, neon, ammonia, methane, sodium, potassium and carbon dioxide. I guess, in theory, discounting the fact you'd die in the process if you took a deep enough breath, you'd start to speak in a high voice. Then again, no one could hear it because there is hardly any atmosphere to transmit the sound.

See? You can't even do a classic sound gag by inhaling some helium and breaking into song.

ABOUT THE AUTHOR

Tom McHale has published eight books to date. During the past 15 years, Tom has published nearly 2,000 articles across a variety of publications.

Prior to his writing career, Tom spent 25 years working in the technology industry as a marketing executive. Tom is a graduate of Emory University with a major in Economics and a minor in Computer Science. He completed his Master's Degree in Business Administration at the University of North Florida with a concentration in Finance and Marketing.

tom-mchale.com

ALSO BY TOM MCHALE

The Practical Guide to the United States Constitution

The Practical Guide to Concealed Carry

The Practical Guide to Guns and Shooting, Handgun Edition

The Practical Guide to Reloading Ammunition

The Practical Guide to Gun Holsters for Concealed Carry

www.ingramcontent.com/pod-product-compliance
Lightning Source LLC
Chambersburg PA
CBHW060452030426
42337CB00015B/1555